The saints are a rebuke and a challenge hardly to be suffered, for their way is always the impractical way of the Sermon on the Mount: poverty, humility, the following of the Cross. And yet, when the years move on and we look back, we find that it is not the social reformer or the economist or even the church leader who has done tremendous things for the human race, but the silly saints in their rags and tatters, with their empty pockets and their impossible dreams.

—Caryll Houselander

SAINTS AND HEROES FOR KIDS
Revised and Expanded Edition

Ethel Pochocki

ST. ANTHONY MESSENGER PRESS

Cincinnati, Ohio

RESCRIPT

In accord with the *Code of Canon Law*, I hereby grant my Permission to Publish *Saints and Heroes for Kids*, by Ethel Pochocki.

Most Reverend Carl K. Moeddel
Vicar General and Auxiliary Bishop
of the Archdiocese of Cincinnati
Cincinnati, Ohio
September 30, 2004

Permission to Publish is a declaration that a book or pamphlet is considered to be free of doctrinal or moral error. It is not implied that those who have granted the Permission to Publish agree with the contents, opinions or statements expressed.

Cover and book design by Mark Sullivan
Interior art by Mary Beth Owens

Library of Congress Cataloging-in-Publication Data

Pochocki, Ethel, 1925-
    Saints and heroes for kids / Ethel Pochocki.—Rev. and expanded ed.
        p. cm.
    ISBN 0-86716-554-5 (alk. paper)
    1. Christian saints—Biography—Juvenile literature. 2. Heroes—Biography—
Juvenile literature.   I. Title.
    BX4658.P628 2005
    282'.092'2—dc22

2004024254

ISBN 0-86716-554-5
Copyright ©2005, Ethel Pochocki. All rights reserved.
Published by St. Anthony Messenger Press
28 W. Liberty Street
Cincinnati, OH 45202-6498
www.AmericanCatholic.org
Printed in the U.S.A.

05 06 07 08 09 10 9 8 7 6 5 4 1

TABLE OF CONTENTS

Introduction   vii

Saint Martin of Tours (316–397)   1

Saint Brigid (c. 525)   7

Saint Margaret of Scotland (1050–1093)   12

Saint Hildegarde the Abbess (1098–1179)   18

Saint Thomas Becket of Canterbury (1118–1170)   19

Saint Juan Diego (1474–unknown)   27

Saint Thomas More (1478–1535)   31

Saint Teresa of Avila (1515–1582)   39

Saint Philip Neri (1515–1595)   44

Saint Francis de Sales (1567–1622)   52

Saint Germaine (1579–1601)   57

Saint Rose of Lima (1586–1617)   61

Saint Joseph of Cupertino (1603–1663)   66

Blessed Kateri Tekakwitha (1656–1680)   72

Blessed Junipero Serra (1713–1784)   81

Saint Benedict Joseph Labre (1748–1783)   88

Saint Pierre Toussaint (1776–1863)   92

Saint Rose Philippine Duchesne (1788–1852)   96

Venerable Anne-Therese Guerin (1798–1856)   101

Blessed Damien of Molokai (1840–1889)   106

Saint Katharine Drexel (1858–1955)   114

Saint Josephine Bakhita (1870–1947) 122

Venerable Solanus Casey (1870–1957) 128

Pope John XXIII (1881–1963) 135

Saint Teresa Benedicta of the Cross (Edith Stein) (1891–1942) 142

Saint Maximilian Kolbe (1894–1941) 147

Dorothy Day (1897–1980) 157

Caryll Houselander (1901–1954) 162

Blessed Teresa of Calcutta (1910–1997) 171

Archbishop Oscar Romero (1917–1980) 178

Four Women Martyrs of El Salvador 185
 Dorothy Kazel (1939–1980)
 Jean Donovan (1953–1980)
 Ita Ford (1940–1980)
 Maura Clarke (1931–1980)

Saint Gianna Molla (1922–1962) 194

Doctor Thomas Dooley (1927–1961) 200

Father Mychal Judge (1933–2001) 209

Sister Thea Bowman (1937–1990) 215

The Holy Innocents of 9/11 221

INTRODUCTION

The trouble with a book like this is that it's never finished. I'm never satisfied. I start out with a definite idea of the kind and number of saints I hope to make come alive. Favorites rise quickly, crowd together, wait in line, eager to jump onto the paper and tell their stories. I think I'll have no trouble at all, that I know *exactly* how it will turn out.

Then I begin my research, cover the table with books and magazines and papers, and as I work away, before I know it, I've discovered and gotten hooked on a saint I've never heard of and must know more about, a saint who is so funny, brave, outrageous or noble that I *must* include him or her in the book. This happens again and again. One saint leads to another and yet another. It's like eating peanuts and potato chips: You just have to have one more...and then another.

This book can only be a sampling of those wonderful saints and heroes who have lived and struggled as we do. They used God's grace and guidance so wholeheartedly that they inspire us still. If they rose above and converted their challenges, so can we! They are the road-markers for us as we meander, spurt, stumble, dance or career down our own particular paths. They even glow in the dark, which is very helpful since that's where a lot of us are much of the time.

Since I was limited by time and space, I chose the saints and heroes I feel are especially meaningful for our lives today. They are my personal choices, and I'm sorry if some of *your* favorite people are not included. I haven't separated the saints from the heroes. They are mixed together here, as I'm sure they are in heaven. My feeling is that canonization is an earthly celebration for us humans. We need to see proof, like the apostle Thomas who had to stick his fingers in Jesus' wounds. God, who knows us by name and has set a seal upon us, already knows the truth and extent of our holiness.

This gathering of holy ones spans twenty centuries, yet their circumstances and problems mirror ours today. They too wrestled with problems of war and ethics, commitment and service, right thinking and wise acting. They worked at how best to love God and their neighbor, even to the point of giving their lives for both.

Among this varied bunch we have soldiers and sailors, kings and queens, doctors, lawyers, beggars, thieves, poets, diplomats, fools and cranks. Some saints helped the homeless and helpless and some *were* homeless and helpless. Some have added to the world's store of truth and beauty with their words and music. Some are martyrs who have given witness by their deaths. Some saints died young while others lived into their nineties.

They are men and women of all nationalities, races and personalities, all part of that wonderful, marvelous mystery we know as the Mystical Body of Christ. If PBS were to televise a special on the Mystical Body, I wonder how they would portray it. Would they show it as a living, throbbing physical body, crisscrossed with roadmap veins and arteries? Or would they show it as a community, a country, a *universe* alive with incredible complementary colors and one-of-a-kind souls, each offering a unique contribution to the whole?

We may not like some of the offerings; we can't like everyone. Sometimes it's hard to understand why some people become saints. As carefully as we try to put together the jigsaw of their lives, to figure out why some who were once mean, selfish or frivolous became heroically holy, generous and compassionate, there is always one piece missing. That piece is a mystery. We don't really *know* why bad people become good, or how the spark of God's grace catches and consumes a soul. But God knows, and eventually so will we.

The important thing to remember is that saints were human. Phyllis McGinley writes in her book *Saint Watching*, "They lost their tempers, got hungry, scolded God, were egotistical or testy or impatient in their turns, made mistakes and regretted them. Still they went on doggedly, blundering toward heaven...."

May the saints and heroes in this book help us all to keep on blundering toward heaven!

MARTIN OF TOURS

There once was a boy named Martin who thought the most important thing in the world was to do one's duty and to do it *well*. If you were a tailor, you should sew seams straight as an arrow. If you were a gardener, you should plant your cabbages when maple leaves were the size of squirrels' ears. If you were a soldier, as Martin was, you should be fearless and sit proudly on your fine horse, your shield burnished and your helmet's plume straight and tall.

Martin was a soldier because his father was a soldier. He was born in an army camp in the outpost of Hungary, and he grew up with the sounds of legions marching and changing guard. He did not particularly want to be a soldier, but his father told him it was the right thing to do. He felt a duty to respect his father's wishes and so, at the age of fifteen, Martin jointed the imperial cavalry. It would not be an unpleasant life, he thought. He loved horses and order and precision.

Martin eagerly listened as his friends in the barracks discussed Christian ideas. He learned of Christ and the message that all people are brothers and sisters. The more he thought about it, the more he knew he would become a

Christian. Someday. Someday soon. Maybe tomorrow. But definitely not today.

Martin was a good soldier who spared himself nothing in work or bravery, and within three years he had become leader of his battalion. He cut a handsome figure as he rode ahead of his men—tall, blond, blue eyes that looked directly at you when he spoke. His words were gentle, even when giving orders.

One winter his unit was transferred to France, to a city named Amiens. It was the bitterest of cold days and Martin took on the extra job of inspecting the stables and food supplies so his men could have some relief from the cold. As he rode his horse past the gate into the city, he saw a huddled mass of rags and flesh. The bare skin of the man's bony arms was turning purple, and he shivered as he shakily held a bowl out for whatever food he could beg from passersby.

No one stopped. It was much too cold to stay out longer than one had to in such weather. The crowd scurried past and hurried to return to the warmth of their homes. Martin, too, passed by, but he thought, "How can I do this? This poor man is my brother. How can I think noble thoughts about loving my neighbor if I go past this beggar and pretend I don't see him? Am I a Christian or not?"

He turned his horse around and went back to the beggar. He knew he had no food or money with him, so he took off his heavy, warm cloak made of red wool and neatly split it in half with his sword. Then Martin wrapped it snugly around the speechless man's shoulders and put the other half around his own. "We are brothers, my friend," he said gently. "This belongs to you as well as me."

Martin rode off and came smack up against his commanding officer. He stared at Martin with angry surprise and then scolded him for destroying government property. "Why did you do such a ridiculous thing?" he demanded. Martin said nothing in his defense because he knew the officer was not a Christian and would not understand.

That night Martin had a dream that was so real it woke him up. In his dream he saw Christ wearing the half-a-cloak he had given the beggar. The Lord was surrounded by angels who asked him where he had gotten such a fine garment. "From my servant Martin, who has not yet been baptized," he said.

When Martin woke, he dressed quickly and ran through the quiet morning streets, searching for the first priest he could find in Amiens. When he was baptized, he felt a great joyful peace. *Someday* had finally become *today*. "I'm a Christian," he sang to himself. "Because of that," he thought, "I shall make an even better soldier."

For two years he tried to be an even better soldier but found that he no longer felt proud of a life of fighting and killing and burning homes and lands. He went to his commander, Julian, and asked to be released from the Roman army.

Julian became very angry and yelled loudly that Martin was a coward and a weakling. This hurt Martin, because he knew he had never been either, but he knew that Julian was upset by other things such as the battle brewing against the Allemani, a savage tribe crossing the Alps from Italy and spreading all over France.

When Martin refused to fight, Julian had him arrested with the promise that after the battle Martin would be put to death (if he were still alive.) At that moment, a group of Allemani captains came to Julian's tent asking for peace on his terms. Julian, completely surprised, accepted their offer and the battle was never fought.

Deep down, Julian admired Martin's honesty in following the path that was right for him, and he ordered the prisoner's chains removed. "I do not know your Christ," he said to Martin, "but if he is so important to you that you would risk your life to follow him, then you are free to do so."

Martin left the army and became a priest. He traveled throughout the empire, up and down the Alps, eluding robbers and wild animals and avalanches. He preached to wild tribes who would just as soon kill him as a bear for supper. Martin's first job was to get their attention long enough to convince them he was not as tasty as bear. *Then* he could tell them about God and loving one another.

These people were very suspicious and whispered behind their hands to one another while Martin was talking. In one town, everyone worshipped a huge ancient pine tree with its gnarled limbs reaching up to heaven. The people found it easier to adore a tree they could see than a God they could not.

The tree *was* beautiful—proud and towering—and Martin could understand why they were in awe of it. "It is truly a thing of beauty," Martin said to them, "but all things of beauty come from God." So God, not the tree, should be worshipped. If they wouldn't agree to that, then he would cut down their tree.

Angered by such talk, the men came after Martin with thick splintery clubs and pointed rocks. They agreed to cut down the tree themselves, if Martin would stand beneath it. (They were willing to sacrifice their sacred tree if they could be rid of Martin as well.) Martin agreed. He said to them, "Peace, my brothers. I know God is here today. Tie me to the tree. Then cut it down. If I am wrong, then it will crush me."

They thought about this and then said, "All right, but you'll be sorry." Everyone *knew* the tree could fall only one way, and Martin was on that side of the tree. They tied him taut to the tree, and four men took turns chopping the thick trunk. It fell with a cracking, thundering crash—the *other* way, with Martin on top of it! The people were dumbfounded and readily agreed to follow a God who could change the way a tree fell.

Soon Martin became so famous as a holy man that everyone in France wanted him to become the bishop of Tours. This was the last thing Martin wanted. After all these years of teaching and preaching, he wanted to build a hut in the forest and spend the rest of his life serving God in prayer and simplicity.

But he knew he had to do what God called him to do. He would have to wait to plant his peas and thatch his roof and pray while the wild cuckoo sang in the night. He would be bishop for as long as the people needed him. But he continued to live a simple life.

His training as a soldier helped him to be on time, to work quickly to take care of his many duties and to be fearless in confronting evil. Although he would never again go into battle as a soldier, he often wrestled with the devil, who teased him in all manner of disguises.

Once when Martin had set out by foot for Rome, the devil decided to tag along, darting in and out of his path like a bothersome fly. "Oh me, oh my, could this be Bishop Martin, the bishop of Tours, *walking*? Like an ordinary beggar? Oh, the shame of it! It cannot be, I must be wrong!"

Martin would not be rattled. "You are too smart to be wrong, Devil. Now what are you up to today? What is it you want?"

"Well, I just cannot *imagine* a bishop being so poorly treated. Surely your Master should do better for you. At least give you a horse, like the good old days. It's a long, dusty way to Rome, you know."

"Yes, I know," said Martin smiling. "What I need is a good old mule." With that, he pointed his finger at the devil and changed him into a donkey on the spot. He climbed on his back and said, "Giddap, Devil, see if your feet are as quick as your tongue!"

And off they cantered on that long, dusty road to Rome. The devil was soon sweating and panting, and by the time they reached the city, he was ready to collapse. Martin said good-day to him. "I'm sure I'll see you again. In the meantime, you better rest up. You're in *terrible* shape!"

Martin eventually got his wish to become a hermit. He went to live in a cave, eating simply once a day and sharing his life with anyone who passed his way. When he died, his friends laid his body on a boat without oars or sails and floated it up the river to Tours. It is said that flowers along the riverbank bowed down as the boat sailed by.

BRIGID

Long ago in the early days of Ireland, nearly all the people worshipped nature instead of God. They considered the sun and the moon and oak trees and mistletoe and mushrooms to be gods themselves instead of gifts from God. The leaders of these people were called Druids. Now and then a few hardy Christians popped up, but when they were found out, they became slaves to the Druids.

One of these slaves was a girl named Brigid, who was so full of charm that no one could refuse her anything. She could have been a Druid priestess or Queen of Wild Things or a court magician if she had not been a Christian. But she *was* a Christian, and all her marvelous adventures happened because she loved God and was fearless about doing his will. Brigid was stubborn as well as brave and would not accept a "No" from anyone if she thought the Lord wanted a "Yes."

She had been born to a Christian slave named Brocessa and a wealthy pagan chieftain named Dubhthach. When Brigid was still a baby, her mother was sold to a Druid in Connaught, which was several mountains away from where Brigid remained with her father. Although Brigid was a slave, she was accepted as a member of her father's family and handled many of the household duties.

Brigid was small and graceful, with blond hair and green eyes that danced and laughed. She got away with the most outrageous things. Her worst fault, in her father's eyes, was the way she gave everything away. When the poor came to the door asking for food, she emptied the shelves. She never refused anyone and she never ran out of food because the shelves would fill up as soon as they became bare.

Dubhthach knew this. Still, it angered him that she thought so little of his goods that she would give them to any beggar who asked. Did the girl have no pride or loyalty?

The day she gave away his new wool cloak with the blue velvet lining he became so annoyed that he decided to sell her to King Dunlang. Brigid understood and was sorry, but she couldn't change her ways. She saw our Lord in every poor person and she would never turn our Lord away.

They rode in silence to the palace in her father's chariot, and her father told her to wait—just to sit there and wait, not to do anything. While she tried to do this, a leper came to the carriage asking for money. She had none, so she reached over and gave him Dubhthach's sword, laden with jewels, and the leper hobbled off quickly, happy with his good fortune, afraid she would change her mind.

When Dubhthach returned and saw what had happened, he turned purple with anger and sputtered, "This is positively the last straw!" He dragged her into the court and pushed her before the king.

He explained why he was here, ending with "You see, Your Highness, this ungrateful girl has just given away my jeweled sword, which you yourself gave me. There is no end of trouble with this girl!"

The king looked at Brigid and smiled on the inside, even

though he tried to frown on the outside. Such an innocent, wide-eyed, loving face looked back at him, with not a bit of remorse! "Why did you do this, Brigid?" he asked.

"If I had my way," answered the girl, "I would give everything to anyone who asked, for God asks this of us. Just as God gives so much to us freely, so should we give."

The king, who was a Christian, understood. He turned to Dubhthach and said, "I cannot purchase your daughter because she is too precious for the gold and silver I own. Let her go to choose her own life, and then you will be free of her." He told Brigid she was no longer a slave and then gave Dubhthach a sword finer than he had before.

And so Brigid set off to find her mother, walking the long distance to the home of the Druid who owned her. When they were reunited, they were so happy that Brigid decided to stay and help her mother. They tended the cattle, milked the cows and made butter and cheese. Things were fine until Brigid started giving away food again.

As in her father's house, the more she gave away, the more the milk and butter increased. At first the Druid owner and his wife were angry. Then, when they saw how much their food increased, they were certain Brigid had magical powers with the animals. They respected her as if she were one of their own priestesses and tried to give her a herd of cattle. Brigid asked for her mother's freedom instead, and she got it.

She went back to visit Dubhthach and found that he had a would-be husband waiting for her. After all, he said, she was still his daughter and he wanted to be sure she would marry the proper kind of young man. He had chosen a well-known young poet.

Brigid replied that the poet was probably a *very* nice person, but she could not consider it. She said she had chosen the Lord as her husband.

Dubhthach refused to hear such nonsense and said yes she *would* marry the poet, and that was that. When Brigid went to bed that night, she prayed the Lord would take away her beauty, and how he did! The next morning one of her eyes had become large and swollen, the other small and squinty. Her lovely hair had become stringy and scraggly, and a big red boil sat on the end of her nose. No one could stand to look at her, so her father gladly gave her the freedom to give herself to Christ.

Brigid and seven of her friends traveled to Croghan Hill where they professed their new life to God in front of Bishop Mel. A pillar of fire is said to have shone about Brigid's head, which so rattled the bishop that he said the wrong prayers and made her a bishop by mistake!

Then another marvelous thing happened. As Brigid bent to receive her veil, she took hold of the wooden altar rail, which was smooth and polished as fine furniture, and it turned fresh and alive and sprouted leaves, until there grew a lovely bower of green all around her. Her ugliness disappeared and she was as beautiful as she had ever been.

Brigid founded an abbey at Kildare, and it became a real community, with priests and artists and poets and scholars living together. It grew large enough to become a town with its own bishop, and Brigid went off in her chariot to all corners of Ireland, telling about Christ and charming the people and making them smile with her daring. She had so many adventures and escapes and crash-ups in her chariot that everyone cleared the road when they knew Brigid was coming. She was rather a reckless driver, counting on the Lord to keep her in one piece for as long as he needed her.

Once when she heard that a poor man had been unfortunate enough to kill the king's pet wolf by mistake, she jumped into her chariot to go to the king and plead with him to spare the man's life. The wolf had been the king's joy, so tame he would lie by the king's feet and roll over and do tricks for him. Now the wolf was dead, and the king's anger was great.

As the chariot raced to the palace, a huge white wolf bounded alongside and finally jumped in beside Brigid. "Well, what have we here?" she gasped, as the wolf started to lick her face with his large red tongue. "Have you been sent from heaven, my friend?"

The wolf laid his chin on her shoulder and grinned, with his tongue hanging out of his mouth.

When they arrived at the palace, he walked beside her, as well-behaved as if he had always visited the palace. They went before the king and bowed long before him. The wolf lay down and covered his eyes with his paws.

"Your Highness," said Brigid, "I have come to ask that you spare that poor fellow's life. He did not kill your dear pet on purpose. And see what I have brought you! Another wolf, grand and smart, and with such a beautiful white coat!" The wolf jumped up and went to the king and put his wet nose in the king's hand.

The king's anger melted and he laughed. The court had never heard him laugh so early in the morning, so this was a good sign. He granted the man a pardon, not only because he was so pleased with the wolf, but also because he could not deny Brigid what she asked.

It was said of Brigid, "She dips her fingers in the stream and the ice melts. She breathes upon the world and the winter is gone." Her warmth made the world she lived in a sunny, comfortable place to be. The doors to her monastery and her heart were always open, and every visitor made welcome.

Be careful if you open *your* heart and let her in. She will take it and run straight away with it to God.

MARGARET OF SCOTLAND

Once upon a time there was a beautiful princess named Margaret who lived a fairytale life in the royal court of Hungary and loved every minute of it. She had everything to make her happy—parents who loved her, dolls, a crown with rubies, a jump rope and her own pony. She ate from white porcelain dishes with roses and crowns painted along the edges and wore petticoats of lace made by nuns in French convents.

She learned Latin and Greek and how to address the king of Germany, for one day she would be queen and need to know these things. Indeed, one day she did become queen, not of her native Hungary but the faraway land of Scotland. It was something she never expected. Here the fairytale life turned into a marvelous adventure.

When she was twelve, she set off with her father, Edward Aethling, a prince of England, and her mother, sister and brother, to visit her granduncle, King Edward. They stayed there several years until the king died. Since they didn't want to get caught in the war going on there between the Normans and the Saxons, they thought it was time to go home. So they packed up their trunks and boarded a ship that would take them to Hungary.

But a wild, blustery storm came up and blew them off course, up into the North Sea and onto the coast of Scotland. The battered vessel, grounded in a cove, was sighted by Malcolm Canmore, a burly boulder of a man who was king of Scotland. He and his warriors were ready to do battle with the unknown sailors of the strange ship, their bows and arrows at the ready for the command to shoot. But the order never came, for Malcolm had spied the three women on deck and found one of them especially lovely.

Malcolm welcomed the weary passengers and took them to live in his castle at Dunfermline. Everything here was so different from the refinement and gracious manners that Margaret took for granted. The weather was harsh and brooding and grim, and the people seemed to take after the weather.

The fierce, rough, quick-tempered Malcolm had lost his heart to the young princess and tried his best to curb his ways and woo her the way a gentleman would. He finally persuaded her mother that Margaret should be his queen. After getting her blessing, he proposed to Margaret, who said she had to think about it.

Margaret knew that such a marriage would bring a hard life in an alien land and a busy social life. She yearned for a quiet life of prayer, and she and her sister, Christina, wanted to enter a Benedictine monastery. Still, she felt that God might want her to marry Malcolm, even though it meant giving up her dream of life as a nun. She realized that as queen she could do much good for the poor people of the country. And so she put her doubts behind her and said yes to Malcolm.

So began the life of Queen Margaret. The people called her Margaret the Good. She took on her job with quiet determination. Malcolm was a great leader and fighter but not much of a scholar or philosopher. He fought the wars and Margaret ruled at home. Her country was in terrible shape.

Robbers took over highways. Neighbors were suspicious of each other and didn't care about anyone but themselves. Peasants (often captured prisoners from England) were treated like slaves. Orphans begged in the streets. There were few schools or hospitals.

Margaret had her work cut out for her. She thought, "Well, if I'm queen, then I must act like one. If God is with me, nothing shall daunt me. I will clean up this place!"

First she decided people feared what they did not know. If they could read, they would understand these things and no longer fear them. She built schools and taught the priests how to read so they in turn could teach their flocks. She started hospitals and homes for the disabled and elderly. She herself served hot soup in the kitchens opened to the hungry.

Margaret had been brought up in a Roman Christian culture in Hungary. She discovered that many of the priests in Scotland kept to the old Celtic Christianity and celebrated Mass and the feasts in their own way. They continued many of the old pagan blessings and brought their love for the natural world into Christianity. They found the world a place of

beauty, a gift to be embraced rather than rejected.

Their monasteries were independent centers of culture and art as well as spiritual centers, and the abbot was the holy ruler. There was no title higher than abbot—even Christ was known as the "Abbot of the Blessed in Heaven." Each monastery went its own way with its own rules, without ever a thought of another "abbot" in a faraway country telling them how to live.

Margaret had to use all her persuasion and diplomacy to join the Celtic and the Roman ways, so that neither side felt it was giving in. She did not frown or decree or demand that they do as she said because she was the queen. Instead she reasoned sweetly with them, showing them that if they truly wished to follow our Lord's example, they would study and learn the gospel. The priests listened and felt the truth in her wise words and agreed that they would.

Margaret was a gracious queen who loved to make her guests feel at home. There were always fresh flowers on the table for royal dinners and the water in the crystal goblets was icy cold. Her children always waited for their mother to take

the first bite before they touched their food, even if their stomachs were growling. And they hardly ever squirmed in their chairs waiting to be excused.

Margaret was strict with her children, and their days were filled with chores and lessons. But they were not long-faced or grumpy about it. Margaret was such a happy person to be around, she made every chore seem like an adventure. They helped her take care of the sick, carrying pots of chicken soup and pans of scones into the cottages. They visited the elderly and listened to their stories, even thought they had heard them many times before. And they shared their home, the castle, with those who were less fortunate. Every morning Margaret brought nine orphans into the castle, fed them, bounced them on her knee, and hugged and kissed them as she did her own.

To the world she was a great queen without a care in her life. She introduced ferries and foreign trade and tartans to Scotland. But to God and herself, she was Malcolm's wife and the mother of their eight children. Malcolm and Margaret never lost their love for each other, even though they may seem an unlikely pair. He never learned to read, so Margaret taught him all she knew about the world and about God. He would go to church with her and, often at night, they would kneel down and pray together. He loved her so much he would secretly take her books away and then return them covered with jewels, just because he knew how much she treasured them.

Their children turned out as well as any mother could hope. Three sons became kings of Scotland and two became monks. One daughter married King Henry I of Scotland and became Good Queen Maud. Margaret's eldest son died with his father at the Battle of Alnwick. Being a good mother was the key to Margaret's holiness.

Margaret became a saint simply by doing what God called her to do. She did not join a monastery or live in the hermit's hut or become a missionary to the lepers because that was not God's will for her. She was happy being a queen and a mother. She did that so well that you can imagine how royally she must have been welcomed to heaven!

Hildegarde of Bingen was an eleventh-century abbess of a Benedictine abbey in Germany. She was a woman who loved earth as much as heaven, a poet and writer of books on medicine and natural history, an herbalist, musician and composer of sacred church music, which she said was "a symbol of harmony which helps man build a bridge of holiness between this world and the World of all Beauty and Music." In one of her compositions, she compares herself to a feather dancing on the breath of God.

"I dance as a feather
on the breath of God"
she sang, then spun
like milkweed down
to the courtly tune
He whistled

whither He blew,
her soul flew free
over rocks and stars
and almond trees,
in scarlet shoes
she danced and danced
upon the Piper's will

and when at last
He caught His breath
and no thing stirred at all,
she fell in pliant curtsy,
waiting to resume

THOMAS BECKET OF CANTERBURY

Once there was a young man who was impetuous, quick-tempered, and who always had to have the last word. He loved the good life and did everything in a spectacular way. He was smart and sharp and clever. He was a lawyer, the king's chancellor and the second most powerful man in twelfth-century England.

There didn't appear to be a holy bone in his body. God, of course, knew better. He knew that under all the glittery, frivolous surface, Thomas Becket of Canterbury had the makings of a martyr and a saint.

There are two stories about Thomas's parents. One, the more romantic, is that his mother was a beautiful Saracen princess who met his father, a crusader in the Holy Land, and fell in love with him. After the Crusades, he returned to England, and she followed him, searching through Europe, knowing only two words of English: *London* and *Becket*.

Against all odds, she did find him! She became a Christian, they married, had a son and lived a happy, comfortable life in London.

The other story is that his parents, Gilbert and Matilda Becket, had come to London from Normandy. Gilbert became a prosperous tradesman and eventually sheriff or mayor of London. They too lived a comfortable, happy life.

We don't know which story is true, but we do know that Thomas was an attractive, charming, quick-witted young man. Whenever he saw an opportunity to better himself or gather praise for his deeds, he grabbed it.

On his walks with his father around London, he took note of all the bright, wonderful things sold at the market: gold and silver watches and goblets, carved furniture, polished armor, furs and peacock plumes. He was attracted by anything dazzling and dramatic. Some day, he resolved, he would own such things. He would wear ermine and carry a silver sword and own falcons.

After finishing high school at Merton's Priory in Surrey, he continued studying in Paris, where he became a skilled debater. By the time he was twenty-four, his cleverness and charm caught the attention of Theobald, archbishop of Canterbury, and Thomas was given a job in his household. Realizing that the young man was a bright scholar, Theobald sent Thomas to Bologna, Italy, to study civil and church law. After he returned, Thomas was appointed archdeacon of Canterbury.

It was at this time, in the course of his duties, that he met Henry II, king of England. Although Thomas was fourteen years older than Henry, the two became best friends and kindred spirits. They were as close as brothers. They went hunting and hawking together, sang, drank, outdid each other in wild stories and foolish pranks.

The friendship was surprising because the two men were so

different, except that they both had terrible tempers and did things on impulse. Thomas had all the social graces Henry lacked. The king loved to hunt deer and wild boar and loved the physical challenge of sports. He dressed sloppily and couldn't be bothered to be polite. When he went to church, he paid little attention to what was going on at the altar, preferring either to talk or draw pictures on his hymnal.

Yet, in spite of everything, people said that Henry and Thomas had but one mind and one heart.

When Thomas was thirty-seven, Henry appointed him chancellor of England. Now he had everything he wanted: money, position and power. All his dreams of living in pomp and style could come true.

Thomas entertained lavishly, even when he was traveling. On one trip to France to arrange a royal wedding, he took with him two hundred knights, esquires, musicians, singers, eight wagonloads of presents, hawks, hounds, monkeys and casks of wine and beer. "If this be the chancellor's state," the French gasped, "what can the king's be like?"

In a few years, when Theobald died, Henry wanted to make Thomas archbishop of Canterbury, but Thomas said, "No. Should God permit me to be an archbishop, I should soon lose your majesty's favor, and the affection with which you now honor me would turn to hatred. For the things you do in prejudice to the rights of the Church make me fear you would require of me what I could not agree to."

Thomas knew that the king wanted him to be archbishop not only because of their friendship but also so Thomas would then be the king's man and must go along with whatever he wanted done. Thomas knew that if he were an honest archbishop, he would have to be God's man first.

The king would not listen to Thomas's protests. "Nonsense, nothing could ever change our friendship. And you *will* be the archbishop of Canterbury!"

Thomas consented and resigned his chancellorship. He was ordained a priest the day before he was consecrated archbishop. From that day, things were never the same between the two strong-willed men.

At that time in England, there was a conflict between the government and the church. The church claimed it governed the lives of priests completely and anything that "pertained to the souls" of the laity. It also declared that the king could not touch matters that involved church property. In other words, the pope, not the king, was the head of the church, and Thomas was determined to keep it that way.

Right before Henry's eyes, Thomas began to change. Henry realized that he hadn't truly been of one mind and one heart with his friend after all, that a steel core of piety and ethics lay beneath Thomas's charming ways. It annoyed Henry to see the archbishop's manner of living change. There were no more lavish parties, no fancy dress. Thomas now wore a simple black cassock with white surplice. He fasted and got up in the night to pray and do penance. He gave alms every morning at ten, generously and personally, and was genuinely concerned about the monks who worked for him.

Henry was baffled, then angry, at his friend's new way of life. After all, he had made Thomas the second most powerful person in the realm, and *this* was how he was repaid? What crazy thinking had changed him into this simpleminded monk who did everything "for God's honor"?

Henry set out to test Thomas and began making laws against the church. Thomas opposed him most of the time but feared going too far. Once he weakened and gave in to signing the Constitutions of Clarendon, which denied the clergy the right of trial by church court and prevented them from making a direct appeal to the pope.

In remorse, Thomas later regretted doing this. "I am a proud, vain man," he said sadly, "a feeder of birds and a follower of hounds, and *I* have been made a shepherd of sheep...." Admitting his mistake, he turned around and rejected the Constitutions. As he had foreseen, the friendship between king and archbishop began to turn to hatred.

Henry ordered Thomas to turn over his church accounts. Thomas refused and encouraged other bishops not to comply with the order. Henry tried to imprison Thomas, but Thomas escaped to France, where he lived in exile for six years at the Abbey of St. Columba, as guest of King Louis VII.

Finally, Henry came to France to patch up his differences with Thomas. Thomas swore an oath of loyalty to his king on all points, save where God's honor came first.

Thomas returned to England, sailing from France to Kent, where the way to the cathedral was lined with cheering people. Every bell in Canterbury was ringing in a joyful clamor. But Thomas found himself in immediate trouble.

He had excommunicated the archbishop of York, one of the king's handpicked men, and others who assisted at the coronation of Henry's son, a ceremony which only the archbishop of Canterbury could perform. The angry bishops hurried to report to Henry what this upstart bishop had done and to warn him that as long as Thomas was around, there would never be peace.

Henry, his patience worn through, flew into one of his tantrums, banging the table with his fists and crying out, "Will no one rid me of this troublesome priest?"

Four of his knights looked at each other, all of one mind. Quietly they withdrew from the room where their monarch still raged, and left for Canterbury. They had taken his harsh words, spoken in anger, as permission to do the deed.

On the afternoon of December 29, Thomas was sitting in his bedroom talking with friends when he received word that the king's knights were there and wished to see him. "When the Church's rights are violated, I await no man's permission to vindicate them. I will give the king the things that are his, but to God, the things that are God's. It is my business and only I shall see to it.... All the swords in England will not frighten me from my obedience to God and my lord, the pope. I gave way once—but never again."

The sullen knights called on the bystanders not to let the archbishop escape. "I am not going to escape," retorted Thomas. "You know where I am." The knights left the room, uttering more threats and shouting, "To arms!"

Thomas sat in silence on his bed. A friend asked him why he had been so headstrong; it served no purpose but to anger the knights further. "I am ready to die," said Thomas calmly, "to die with dignity and for principle. For God's honor."

Then came loud noises from the outside, shouting, crashing, crunching, the breaking down of doors to the cathedral. Thomas got up and walked, by way of a private door, to the church, his attendant carrying the cross before him. Frightened monks, fearful for his life and theirs, met Thomas, and he ordered them back into the choir.

"What are you frightened of?" he asked the quaking crowd which had already gathered for vespers. They cried out, "Armed men, there in the cloisters!" And Thomas saw dimly the shadows of the four knights with weapons drawn. One of them called out, "Where has that traitor Thomas gone?"

Thomas called out from the steps of the choir, "Here I am, no traitor, but archbishop and priest of God. What do you want?" He came down the steps and stood between the altars of our Lady and Saint Benedict.

The knights moved out of the shadows, advancing to the altar, and demanded that he absolve the bishops he had excommunicated. "I cannot do that," he answered. He turned to one of the knights and called him by name, "Reginald, you have received many benefits from me. Why do you come into my church with arms?"

The knight raised his axe in reply. "You shall die! I shall tear your heart out!" The other three joined him and they fell upon and began to hammer and slash and batter the body of the archbishop. In a matter of minutes, Thomas lay on the floor in a crumpled, bloodied heap.

"Into thy hands I commend my spirit," he cried out with the last bit of life, "for the name of Jesus...." To finish him off, the knights attacked and beat him further, until Thomas Becket, archbishop of Canterbury, spoke no more.

The murderers, emboldened by their triumph, rushed off to ransack the archbishop's house, in the hope of finding secret treasure. They found nothing of value, just a few prayer books, two hair shirts and a falconer's glove, given to Thomas by the king. They tossed these things aside in disgust and rode off proclaiming, "The traitor's dead and will rise no more!"

When the king heard the news, he was horrified, especially since he was the cause of this terrible happening. Moaning and crying, he shut himself up in his room and fasted for forty days, and then did public penance at Thomas's tomb. For the rest of his life, his conscience gave him constant reminder of the power of ill-spoken words.

Thomas was declared a martyr immediately by the pope, and three years later, a saint. For nearly three hundred years, Canterbury Cathedral became one of the most sacred places of pilgrimage in the medieval world, until another Henry (the Eighth) ordered the shrine destroyed and the saint's bones burned. Today there is a square stone in the pavement that marks the exact spot where Thomas died, and the pilgrims still come.

Some say that Thomas became a martyr by accident, that death took him as suddenly and impersonally as a terrorist's bomb takes the lives of innocent airplane passengers, or snipers' bullets kill United Nations' peacekeepers and famine relief workers.

But Thomas had a choice in his death. His attendant testified, "The archbishop might easily have saved himself by flight...for it was evening, and the crypt was near at hand, where there were many dark and winding passages, or gone up to the roof of the cathedral by another door." Instead, Thomas did not argue or turn away or yield to force. He accepted death "for God's honor."

Twelfth-century Thomas would easily adapt to today's world. He loved the good life and comfortable living. He was certain that he was right, even though he made mistakes, and he had to have the last word. But with God's grace, he gained the courage to let God have the last word. That should encourage all of us!

JUAN DIEGO

If the story of Our Lady of Guadalupe were a play, Mary would be its star. She would be the center of all eyes, the one with the best dialogue, the artist skilled in turning hearts and changing minds, and the one to get the bouquets at curtain call (roses, of course).

But she wasn't a one-woman show. She needed supporting players—assorted peasants, friars and street people, a Spanish bishop, a dying uncle, and, most importantly, the messenger. Without the messenger, Juan Diego, we would have no Guadalupe. And without the appearance of the Lady at Guadalupe, there would not have been the conversion of nine million Aztecs, who could not resist the message of Mary, who came to them as an Aztec Princess.

Juan Diego must have been exactly right for the role, because he was chosen by the star herself. But what do we know of him beyond this performance? Just a handful of facts. He was born around 1474 and lived in the village of Tolpetlac, with his wife, Maria Lucia. He was a farmer, growing mostly corn, in his Aztec community.

After the Spaniards conquered Mexico in 1521, it was a time of hardship and cruelty for the Aztecs. The Europeans considered them an inferior race, good only for use as slaves. But along with the soldiers, there came good men also, friars, who preached about their God who was a loving father to all. The natives wondered how this compassionate God could be the God of their tormentors as well. Nonetheless, Juan and Maria decided there was truth in what the friars said, and they were baptized in the new faith. They had no regrets for their old life but sometimes they did miss having a dozen gods for different purposes, instead of just One taking care of everything.

When Maria died, Juan was heartbroken, but he believed she was now in Heaven, happy, healthy and waiting for him. He tried to live his life as before, but the house was so lonely without Maria, he moved in with his sick, elderly uncle. It cheered him up to have someone to take care of. As the years passed, Juan Diego became known as an *ancianos*, a wise and kind man venerated by his community.

He was fifty-seven years old when he met Mary for the first time that December morning on his way to Mass. Can you imagine how he felt as he was stopped in his tracks by the brilliant assault of birdsong? When he saw the cloud part to reveal the lovely woman dressed as an Aztec? To be addressed as "Juanito, my son will you deliver a message to Bishop Zumarrago for me?"

Juan thought he was dreaming. Yet, the woman had called him by name. She had been there, real, he could see the color of her eyes. Now she was gone and left him with work to do, and he set off to do it.

His faith was uncluttered with doubt or worries over what people would think. Still, he did not look forward to walking into the bishop's palace and being scorned, laughed at, sent away or thrown out. An Aztec wanting to talk to the bishop about the Virgin Mary. Imagine!

And yet, the bishop *did* speak with him. (A little grace, a nudge, a whisper in the ear, God has his ways.) "I'm busy now," he told Juan. "Come back again and we'll talk about it."

On the second attempt, the Bishop seemed to believe him, but asked for a sign. Poor Juan must have been exhausted, but the Lady said she would have a sign for him. So Juan prepared for the third trip, when his uncle suddenly became very ill and asked for a priest. Juan knew he could not let his uncle down and hoped Mary would understand. He chose a different route in order to avoid her. But there she was, waiting round the bend!

You can't help smiling and feeling sorry for Juan, as he tried to explain and make excuses and even get out of this job he didn't want to do. But Mary just smiled that smile that mothers give when they say no—very sweet and understanding, but firm. She told Juan not to worry about his uncle, he was already healed, and to climb to the top of Tepeyac Hill where he would find the glorious, fragrant Castillian roses growing. Roses in the snow! He was to pick them, as much as he could hold, and give them to the bishop as the sign he wanted.

He trudged off to Mexico City, smelling heavenly of the gift he carried within his *tilma* (cloak). When he stood before the bishop and opened the tilma, an explosion of color and fragrance burst upon the stunned bishop. Roses in December, roses he remembered from his native Spain. This good man was indeed Mary's messenger! And then, another miraculous sign was given—the imprint of Mary as an Aztec woman, Our Lady of Guadalupe, was indelibly and mysteriously painted on the back of Juan's tilma, an imprint that has lasted, unfaded, and is venerated today.

Juan Diego spent the rest of his life taking care of the shrine and then the church which the Bishop built on the spot Mary had chosen, living his quiet simple life, until he joined Maria in Heaven.

So why do we honor this ordinary man as a saint? He was not a martyr, a great thinker, a dazzling preacher, or a hermit who spent his life praying. He was exactly what he seemed, a good man, humble, obedient, and running over with faith, a chosen one, who, like Mary, thrust into extraordinary circumstances, had the courage to say *Yes!*

THOMAS MORE

Saints and heroes seem to like the name *Thomas*. Just look at the ones in this book! Each took very different paths to God. Yet two of these Thomases had much in common.

They were both born in the Cheapside section of London, were pages in the household of the archbishop of Canterbury, studied and practiced law, were well-loved friends and advisors of two King Henrys, fell into disfavor with them and lost their lives for putting God before king. One was Thomas Becket of Canterbury; the other was Thomas More.

Thomas More was born on February 7, 1478, the son of John More, a lawyer, and his wife, Agnes. He was bright and charming with a sunny disposition, the kind of child mothers love to show off with pride. When he was twelve, he was given the honor of being page in the house of the archbishop of Canterbury, where he did so well that he was sent for further education to Oxford at the age of eighteen.

Here he spent two of the most satisfying years of his life. Thomas was a natural scholar, reading every book, soaking up every lecture, reveling in the marvelous worlds his studies opened up to him—astronomy, poetry, philosophy, Latin, Greek. He absorbed knowledge like a thirsty blotter.

He would have been quite content to stay at Oxford and become a scholar and teacher, but instead, encouraged by his father, he went on to study at Lincoln's Inn, London, to become a lawyer. He thrived in this profession and became prosperous and well-known. Since he was quite handsome as well as successful, women had their eyes on him as a great catch.

But Thomas wasn't sure he wanted a wife. For years while he worked at his law practice by day, he lived at a charterhouse of Carthusian monks. He stayed there nights, sleeping on a board with a log for his pillow. He didn't mind such things. He enjoyed the simple, austere life so much he considered becoming a monk. The thought of spending his days in prayer and scholarly things seemed pure joy to him.

But after being honest with himself, getting down to the bare facts as a good lawyer should, he knew the gifts he had been given would be better used in the world. As lawyer and judge, he could help the poor and all those suffering from injustice. And he felt he should marry and have a family, so he could be witness to the noble calling of raising a Christian family. He prayed for the just-right woman.

He found her. Thomas chose for his wife the daughter of a family friend, Jane Colt, a lovely wisp of a girl. She was seventeen and he was twenty-six. Thomas was at first attracted to her younger sister (Jane was the eldest), but as his son-in-law William Roper wrote about Thomas's choice, "When he considered that it would be both great grief and some shame also to the eldest to see her younger sister preferred before her in marriage, he then...framed his fancy toward her, and soon after married her."

Although we may never know Thomas's reason for choosing Jane, we do know theirs was a true love story, but, sadly, short-lived. Jane died in their sixth year of marriage, leaving Thomas with four young children: Margaret, Elizabeth, Cecily and John.

Thomas was grief-stricken. Yet he had to think immediately about the practical matter of caring for his infants. Within a month after Jane's death, he married Alice Middleton, a widow seven years older than he. This may have been a marriage made in necessity, not in heaven, but somehow it worked.

Alice was nothing like sweet Jane. She had blunt and brusque ways and a sharp temper; she loved to gossip, meddle and take charge. But more important, she had a kind heart. Beneath the cackling was a dedicated mother hen.

This didn't mean she didn't get exasperated, for in this household something always set her nerves on edge. For one thing, there was Thomas's menagerie—dogs, cats, birds, rabbits, a fox and a monkey—who had the run of the house. The monkey, who would paw through her clean laundry with dirty paws, was a special source of frustration! Thomas loved animals. He saw them as creatures that glorified God as surely as humans did.

And there were the unexpected guests. They came from all over England and Europe to meet and talk with her brilliant husband and to be charmed by his family. They were always underfoot, eating, laughing, joking, with Thomas the center of their attention—and respect. One of his fellow scholars said, "More is a man of angel's wit and singular learning...a man of marvelous mirth and pastimes, and sometimes of sad gravity. A man for all seasons."

One of the regular guests was the Dutch scholar Desiderius

Erasmus, with whom Thomas formed a deep friendship that is probably still going on. Erasmus said of Thomas the first time they met: "He is so kind...so sweet-mannered that he cheers the dullest spirit and lightens every misfortune. He extracts enjoyment from everything, even from things that are most serious....His face is always...ready to break into smiles."

The More home in Chelsea was surrounded by gardens and groves of lime trees and arbors over which Thomas trained vines to make green, shady tunnels. Rosemary, the herb of friendship, was planted everywhere. And there was a separate building, a chapel and library, where Thomas went to study and pray.

As you can imagine, Thomas was completely content, happy in his work, his family, his home. He became so well-known and admired, however, that he came to the attention of King Henry VIII, who found Thomas more than a match for him in wit and learning, in enjoying poetry and composing music. Above all, Henry had found a man he could trust. The two became strong friends, and the king often showed up unannounced at Thomas's home just to chat and walk, arm in arm, in the gardens. But Thomas never forgot Henry was the king. He told his son-in-law, a bit sadly, "Ah, I tell thee I have no cause to be proud, for if my head would win him a castle in France, it should not fail to go."

After sending Thomas on diplomatic missions to France and Belgium, Henry decided he needed him in the court. Thomas, he declared, would be the Lord Chancellor of England.

Thomas was unwilling. He knew too much about life at court, the cunning and treachery that went on, and he wanted no part of it. He had no craving for power; his reason for being lay in his home at Chelsea. Still, in his heart, he knew he could serve his country well, so he finally accepted, to the delight of his family and his wife, who felt quite puffed up in being the wife of the chancellor of England!

Thomas became even more admired and respected in his new job. God truly used him to help the poor. Thomas set up almshouses and also heard people's complaints and solved them justly. Perhaps, he thought, this would not be as worrisome as he feared.

But then came the problem of Henry's "great matter." The king wished to divorce his wife, Catherine of Aragon. Since he was head of the church of England, which did not allow divorce, the king tried to find some legal way to do this. He claimed his conscience had been troubling him because he had been wrong in marrying his brother's widow, even though he had been granted a dispensation and even a blessing from the pope to do so.

"After all," he explained to Thomas, trying to sound sincere, "even though the pope gave me permission to marry my brother's wife, he is just a man and capable of error, isn't he? To think I may have been sinning all these years.... We must get this marriage annulled for my soul's sake!"

Thomas knew, as did everyone in the court, that Henry's *real* reason was that he wanted to marry Anne Boleyn, a young woman who had taken his fancy.

Thomas tried to avoid giving the king his opinion by saying it was a matter for a priest, not a layperson, to judge. But the king pressed for an answer.

Thomas responded, with reluctance. He said that divorce could not be allowed between those whose marriage had been blessed by the church. Henry's marriage to Catherine was valid and could not be set aside. He declared that since there was a difference between the king and himself, he must resign as chancellor. And he would keep his opinions to himself.

The king was furious. He wanted more than silence; he wanted complete approval, and that Thomas could not give.

The More's family life changed quickly. Now, for the first time, they were poor. Without a salary, they had to dismiss their servants, who left tearfully, for they had been treated as members of the family. Thomas gathered the family together and tried to cheer them up: "May we yet with bags and wallets go a-begging together, and hoping that for pity some good folk will give us their charity, at every mans' door to sing *Salve Regina*, and so still keep company and be merry together!"

For eighteen months they lived this way. In the evenings, the family would gather around the small, single peat fire for prayers and then quickly get into bed in their unheated rooms. It was hard for Thomas to see what his integrity had done to his dear ones, but they, even sharp-tongued Alice, assured him he had done the right thing.

Things got worse when Thomas did not attend Henry's wedding or the coronation of Anne as queen. Then he refused to sign a loyalty oath to the Act of Succession, which stated that the children of Henry and Anne would be rightful heirs to the throne. Out of fear, many Catholics signed it—not to sign would be considered treason—with the reservation "so far it not be contrary to the law of God." Thomas's family signed it and they begged him to, but his conscience would not allow it.

For this he was imprisoned in the Tower of London for fifteen months. What a time of anguish this must have been for him—Thomas More, the prosperous, well-loved scholar, lawyer, family man and, until now, the king's man. Now he sat in his cold cell, isolated, ill, chilled to the bone, worrying about his now-homeless family. (The king had taken Thomas's home and gardens and distributed them among the relatives of Anne Boleyn.)

At first Thomas had been allowed books and pen and paper, visits from his beloved daughter, Margaret, and food that Alice had bought by selling her fine clothes, but soon even those comforts were denied him. He had only one visitor now to cheer him, one of the Tower cats, who would creep in and out the barred windows at will. Thomas would thank the angels for sending her and for a while, purring in his arms, she warmed him, body and soul.

Even though his writing materials had been taken away, Thomas managed to write on a slate with a bit of charcoal a last note to Margaret: "Our Lord bless you good daughter and your good husband and your little boy and also my children. Farewell, my dear child and pray for me and I shall pray for you and all your friends that we may merrily meet in heaven."

Thomas was brought to trial, found guilty of treason and condemned to death. He looked out upon his former friends who had lied and betrayed him out of fear for their lives and spoke gently to them. He would, he said, judge no man's conscience, "which lies in the heart out of my sight." And that even as Paul had persecuted Stephen, "and be they now both ...holy saints in heaven, and shall continue there friends for ever, so I verily trust, and shall therefore right heartily pray, that though your lordships have now here on earth been judges of my condemnation, we may yet hereafter in heaven merrily all meet together to everlasting salvation."

As he was being led back to the Tower, Margaret pushed through the crowds to her father, flung her arms around his neck and kissed and clung to him. Thomas comforted her, "Have patience, Margaret, and trouble not thyself. It is the will of God, my dear child...." The guards pushed her back, she disappeared into the crowd, knowing she would not see him again in this world.

On the morning of his execution, July 16, 1535, he put on his best clothes and walked to the Tower Hill. Even at the scaffold his sense of humor did not fail him as he asked for help from the guard. "I pray thee see me safe up, and for my coming down, let me shift for myself!" he joked with the nervous executioner, trying to put him at ease, and he asked that his beard be spared the axe since *it* was innocent of treason. Then, with one stroke, Thomas More was beheaded.

In all the writings about Thomas, you will find one word above all others that describes him best. It isn't *brilliant, generous, just, kind holy, compassionate,* although he was all of these. It is *merry.* A merry man, the dictionary informs, is one full of cheerfulness, joyous disposition, causing happiness—a perfect description of Thomas More, God's merry man.

TERESA OF AVILA

Once there was a girl named Teresa whose sense of humor was as quick and lively as her dancing feet. She was the kind of girl who got into mischief without even trying to and led others along with her as well. Since she had eleven brothers and sisters, she did not need to look far to round up companions for her adventures.

At age seven, she coaxed her brother Rodrigo to run away with her to Africa where they would instantly become martyrs for Christ. Rodrigo wasn't that excited about becoming a martyr, but such was Teresa's ability to describe the marvelous sights of heaven that he went along anyway.

She ransacked the kitchen and found a sack of raisins, so they might keep up their strength on the way to Africa. They had reached the outskirts of Avila, the town in Spain where they lived, when their uncle found them and brought them home quickly, much to Teresa's annoyance and Rodrigo's relief.

Teresa was dark and pretty, with a mass of dark curly hair, deep brown eyes and a mole, or beauty mark, on her face. She was tall and dimpled and plump.

When she was young, she didn't fast or spend hours on her knees praying. She didn't think much about our Lord at all. Her days were too full of being a young lady. She loved going to dances and bullfights, wearing the latest fashions and perfume. Even the drawers that held her nightclothes were perfumed, so she would smell good even while sleeping.

If she lived today, she would probably go to basketball games and dances, eat hamburgers and drink milkshakes and enjoy every minute of it. She would fit very well into the category we call "normal," with an extra dash of high-spiritedness.

When she was eighteen, something happened inside her soul that only God knows about. Some say reading the letters of Saint Jerome touched off a spark in her heart to give herself completely to God, but it took a while before she gave in to the call to "be perfect." She even prayed to God to please *not* ask her to be a nun. But she knew, even while asking, she would be miserable if she didn't answer *yes* to God's invitation. She later said, "One should not wait until one is perfect or even until one is converted before giving oneself to prayer.... It would be a sad day if we could not draw near to God until we were perfect."

She entered the convent of the Carmelites, and after a time she realized that life there was not very different from the life she had left in the world. Girls came to the convent not so much to love God as to have a comfortable, easy life. They wore jewelry and gave parties and dined on rich foods sent by the girls' families, not just once in a while but all the time. The convent was just another home where girls could do pretty much anything they wanted.

Teresa, who had already known this kind of life, was disturbed in her soul. The Lord told her that this was not right. He wanted her to bring these convents in Spain back to their original simple rule, where the nuns could work and pray and be poor.

This would be a difficult job, and Teresa knelt in her little room and prayed for the courage and wisdom to do it well. She knew what to expect and prepared herself for the outcry. It came.

None of the nuns wanted to change their life of ease. Who was this upstart who, if she had any brains, could have joined their way of life instead of trying to upset it?

The town of Avila turned its back on one of its once-favorite daughters. The nuns and heads of other convents made jokes about her and her foolish mission, and the pope's messenger called her nothing but a gadabout, "The Roving Nun." Some thought it should have been "The *Raving* Nun."

But Teresa went her way. She knew that if God was with her, who could be against her? She traveled about Spain, talking with priests and nuns, trying to coax them to return to the simple life they once knew.

It was not easy for someone used to being popular and the center of attention. She was very much alone. One night in a room above a noisy inn where she had stopped on her journey, she scribbled these lines on a card. It has come to be known as Saint Teresa's bookmark:

> Let nothing disturb you.
> Let nothing affright you.
> All things are passing.
> God only is changeless.
> Patience gains all things.
> Who has God wants nothing.
> God alone is sufficient.

Finally, Teresa received permission to found her own houses according to the original rule. She called the nuns who came to live this rule Discalced Carmelites, which means "those without shoes." They were to be poor, but being poor in things did not mean they were to be dull in spirit. "One does not need shoes to dance," said Teresa, and she gave them proof on the spot!

Teresa went about the country setting up her new convents, traveling by mule cart in scorching heat and freezing cold. She argued her case so charmingly that she won over the archbishop of Seville and even the pope. Teresa was a delight to have around. Often her nuns would beg her to join them in games, and she would get up from her prayers to oblige them. She played the flute and a little drum with bells and, whenever she could, she danced.

She thoroughly enjoyed good food. When her convent was given an unexpected gift of blue cheese or a catch of scallops, she put on an apron and set about immediately cooking up a feast. Once a visitor was shocked to find her happily eating a gift of roast partridge. She had been expecting the great Carmelite Teresa to be existing on bread and water, the way holy people were *supposed* to. Teresa merely licked her fingers, wiped them on her napkin and said, "Let people think what they please. There is a time for penance, and there is a time for partridge. Now is the time for partridge!"

She was like a mother with a large brood of scattered children, grandchildren, sisters, cousins, aunts; she was a shepherdess of a flock of contented lambs and straying black sheep. She praised them, cajoled, scolded and laughed at their antics, and she wrote them letters. Wherever she might rest for the night, she had paper and pen, or sometimes only stubs of pencils, and she wrote.

She sent recipes and advised when to buy plums and grapes at their best price. She lectured kings and consoled bishops.

She admonished her sister for not being a good wife. Always with affection, always with a light, caring touch, she wrote. She loved them all with the same joy. "I have no defense against affection," she said. "I could be bribed by a sardine!"

Teresa could not understand a lack of joy in anyone. "Lord," she said, "deliver me from sour-faced saints!" Even when she was exasperated, she could see the funny side of a situation. Once when her mule cart became mired in the mud and no manner of sweet talk would budge the animal, Teresa looked up to heaven and snapped, "No wonder you have so few friends, when you treat the ones you have so badly!"

She was also a down-to-earth, energetic woman, like a housekeeper who will not be stopped when she decides that the rugs are to be beaten *today*. "Works, no words!" she would say to nuns too wrapped up in holy thoughts to wash the dishes properly. "You can serve God among the pots and pans as well as anywhere else." If anyone complained of her hard life, Teresa would remind her that "those whom His Majesty loves, He treats as He treats His Son."

For all her works as a tireless, optimistic journeyer, she did her finest work for God in prayer. She knew that only by coming close to God could she find the courage to change her world for the better.

Near the end of her life, a priest told her that she was being looked upon as a saint. She, of course, laughed and said, "Father, during my lifetime I have been told I was handsome and I believed it; clever, and I thought it was true; and that I was a saint—but I always knew people were mistaken about *that*."

For once, the joke was on Teresa.

PHILIP NERI

Once upon a time a boy named Philip lived in the city of
Florence, in Italy. He was as bright and warm and handsome
as the city itself. Philip loved Florence. He would lie on a
grassy hill outside the city's walls, watching the sun dance off
the churches' spires and think this must be what heaven is
like. He wanted to be in no other place in the world and no
other person but who he was—a happy boy in a happy family.

His joy in life was catching. He could find absolutely
nothing to frown about, and he could tease a smile from the
most fearful grouch just by the cheerful way he hopped about
like a small sparrow.

Philip did seem more like a sparrow than a boy at times.
Because he was quite frail with brittle bones, his good
stepmother, Maria, sometimes wished she could wrap him in
cotton to protect him. But "Pippi Buono" ("good little Phil"),
as she called him, never minded his banged-up knees or
skinned nose when he fell. He just went his way whistling and
singing, like a sparrow who *will* be cheerful, no matter what.

Most of all, Philip loved to tell riddles, and most of the time his sisters laughed along with him. But sometimes, when he wouldn't stop and kept on and *on*, they would lose their tempers and swat him (but carefully, because he was so little).

He, in turn, could hurt nothing, not even a fly. Once, when a fly fell into his soup and Philip did nothing about it, Maria asked him, "Pippi, what is that fly doing in your soup?" Philip looked at her with innocent brown eyes and said, "The backstroke!" And while they were laughing, he picked the fly out of the bowl before it drowned and let it out the window.

Sparrows must decide which trees to live in and little boys must grow up. When Philip was eighteen, he decided that as much as he did not want to leave his family and his beloved Florence, he must be off to make his own life. He did not want to be a tax collector or a notary like his father, nor did he feel smart enough or good enough to be a priest. Maria, with a mother's special knowing, felt that someday Philip *would* be a priest. But that was in God's hands.

Even though his parents were sad to see Philip leave home, they were happy to know he would be going to live with his Uncle Romolo and Aunt Giovaninni in the town of San Germano, three days away by foot. They wanted him to help in the uncle's business as a merchant. Since Romolo and Giovaninni had no children of their own, Philip would inherit their land and wealth.

So he packed a good hard cheese, a long loaf of garlic bread and some olives in his knapsack and set off for San Germano. He walked all day, enjoying the sun and birdsong and the music of the wind sighing through the fields of wheat. He fell asleep at night under the stars, watching them blink from so far away and still give him comfort. Ah, to be a hermit, to be able to love God without anything getting in the way—this was the life!

When he arrived at San Germano, Philip entered a world far from a hermit's sanctuary. His Uncle Romolo and Aunt

Giovaninni could not do enough for him. He had silk shirts and a belt and shoes with buckles and a bed with a canopy. Best of all, he had the most loving care from his new family. And he, with his charm and sweetness, brought new customers and friends to his uncle's business. It seemed the perfect way to spend a life.

Yet, there was a restlessness in Philip's heart. He had everything. Why was he not satisfied? He spoke of his empty feeling to no one except a monk from a nearby monastery with whom he had become friends. This monk sensed a holiness in Philip that the boy himself did not know. He suggested that Philip make a visit to a shrine at Gaeta, where a rock—said to have split apart on the day Christ died—made a place for a pilgrim chapel.

Philip borrowed a mule from his uncle and started on the day's journey up the mountain. The winds were bitter cold, but Philip whistled cheerfully to calm his fears of slipping on the rocks or getting lost. He finally reached the chapel, and when he entered, he heard nothing of the wind or any other noise from the world outside.

He knelt in the dark and asked, "Lord, here I am. What do you want of me?" and deep in that part of him that was his soul, Philip heard the Lord say, "I have long waited for you to ask me, Philip. I want you to go to Rome, to the city of Peter, and live as a hermit amongst my sick and poor and bring them back to me. You are needed *now*, my Pippi Buono."

> So do not delay,
> Work and pray.
> I will show the way!

Philip felt a rush of warmth wrap around him and carry him up and out of the chapel. When he opened his eyes, he could see the first pink streaks of dawn. He was back in the chapel, on the rock floor. He shook his head to see if anything was loose up there, and then thought about his experience and what he must do. The Lord said he was needed in Rome *now*, so he knew he must set off for that large, unfamiliar city where he knew no one.

But first he must tell his aunt and uncle. Again, he must leave those he had come to love. They tried to make it easier for him, but it was hard for them too. His Uncle Romolo hugged him tightly. "Dear Philip, you would have been a rich man someday if you stayed here, but—I know, you must seek other riches. We shall always love you, and if you wish to return, our arms are open.... Ah well, go in peace."

When Philip reached Rome (it was a long, dusty walk), he was amazed and bewildered. All that noise—men in small huddled groups, children, women, everyone walking, running, yelling, shoving, chasing animals and dodging in and out of doorways. There were all manner of people—beggars, thieves, rich lords and their ladies being carried about in chairs with gold fringe. Philip felt like a flea on an elephant. How was he ever to be a hermit in a place like this? This was a riddle that would take a lifetime to figure out.

He wondered where to go and what to do. He heard that voice deep within him say, "Trust me, Philip, and follow me in all things. I will lead you to heaven, only trust me!"

At that moment, a monk who had noticed the quiet boy came over and asked if he might need a place to stay. Philip nearly jumped out of his skin with joy. "Lord, you certainly do work fast!" he thought. The monk took him to the home of a man called Galeotto del Caccia, who had also been born in Florence. He was a great-sized man, with wealth and generous heart to match, and it pleased him to help this young boy from his hometown.

"Well, young Philip, so you wish to be a hermit? I'm afraid you will have to work at *that* in this city! Even the birds have left for the pine forests so they can hear themselves sing.

However, in the meantime, would an attic room do? It won't be much—a bed, table, chair, a line to hang clothes. And you will eat with us, of course—good plain food, nothing fancy, eggplant, fresh figs...."

Philip couldn't believe his ears. What good fortune! But there was more. "Oh yes, one small thing," Galeotto added. "I would ask you to teach my two sons all the necessary studies for a few hours each morning. Would you be able to do this?"

Would he! Philip was so happy he broke into song. His two new students, Michele and Ippolito, looked at him warily. He was unlike any teacher they had ever known. A little crazy, too, dancing around like that. But maybe he might make studying a bit fun. They wondered if he would last longer than the six previous teachers who had come and gone so quickly!

He did. They got on beautifully. Philip was a born teacher who never appeared to be giving orders. His own enthusiasm for learning rubbed off on the boys, and they met each morning as eager travelers, ready for the day's adventures. Philip had a way of making the most boring arithmetic problem or grammar rules into a game, and he kept their wits sharp with his bag of riddles.

"Now listen to this, Michele: Why isn't your nose twelve inches long? What, you don't know? Then I will tell you. Because then it would be a *foot*!"

Or, he would ask seriously, "When is medicine first mentioned in the Bible?" "When God gave Moses two tablets!"

Or, "What is gray, has four legs and a trunk?" "A mouse going on vacation!"

Or, "What is the smallest room in the world?" "A mushroom!"

Or, "Ippolito, come here. Tell me what kind of tree you have in your hand." And Ippolito would look and look and shake his head, puzzled, until Philip would laugh, "Why, a *palm* tree, of course!"

So the years passed, and Philip's life took him from his attic room hermitage, and the classroom, to the streets of Rome. Here he would stand on street corners and in marketplaces, talking and laughing with all kinds of people, asking them about their lives and hopes. He would tease them good-naturedly about getting to confession and start them thinking about their souls and why they were here on earth. Then he would gather some of his young friends and say, "Well, brothers, when shall we begin to do good?" And they would be off to hospitals to cheer the sick and comfort the sorrowful, begging for food and flowers along the way.

After twenty years of this work, Philip was so well-loved by the people that he became known as the Apostle of Rome. Although they may not have known it at first, he was doing more than making them comfortable in *this* world. He had poked and joked enough to wake up the lazy Christians who had been careless about showing how much they loved God. If they missed Mass and Communion, they just shrugged their shoulders and said, "We'll go tomorrow. There's always tomorrow." Philip made them see that tomorrow never comes, and today, right *now*, was the time to love God.

He decided that he would become a priest so he could hear confessions and bring Communion to all his friends. And so he did, every morning. (He no longer had Michele and Ippolito, who had grown up and become priests themselves.) In the afternoon, he went back to the streets and to those who could not come to him. Some young priests who went with him loved this life so much, they asked if they could all live together as a family.

So Philip sat down and wrote out a set of rules for them, and they prayed and ate and sang and worked together and became known as the Oratorians. This was not because they talked so much (as those of you who have looked up *orator* may think), but because a room has to be built for them in the church of San Girolomo where they could meet, and this room was called the oratory.

Philip's love of justice was as keen as his love of fun. When he gave penances in confession, he made sure that "the punishment fit the crime." Once, a gossip who couldn't stop talking about others came to him. Philip asked her if she would please pluck a goose for him. She thought this a strange penance, but did it nonetheless, all the while chattering to him about the butcher who put sawdust in sausages.

Then Philip told her to carry the pile of feathers to the window and scatter them to the wind. *Very* strange, she thought, but she did this too. The feathers flew in all directions—up, down, onto the clothes on the washline, into the grapevines and even into the ear of the butcher.

"Now," said Philip, "you must catch them and bring back each and every one to me."

"What?" she cried. "Father Philip, you know that is impossible! The wind has taken them into the sky and another country for all I know. You might as well ask me to put them all back on the goose!"

"Exactly," said Philip, "and that is how foolish words, once you speak them, can never be brought back again. They lodge and fester and poison the minds and hearts of all who hear them." The woman was so struck by the truth of his words she promised from then on to speak only good of others, and if what she knew of them was not good, she would not speak at all. Then she hurried off to the butcher's to buy some sausages for supper.

Philip spent thirty more years encouraging and delighting people instead of scolding them, and when he was eighty years old, he left their world for heaven, where he could play his games with a brand-new audience.

He probably asked the Lord right off, "Why did the elephant stand on a marshmallow?" And our Lord, of course, would be too polite to spoil his fun and waited for Philip to answer: "So he wouldn't fall into the cocoa!"

FRANCIS DE SALES

Once upon a time in the town of Sales, France, a son was born to a noble and wealthy family, and they called him Francis in honor of the little saint of Assisi. It seemed a happy omen to his parents that in the room where he was born, there hung a picture of this saint preaching to the birds and fishes.

He was much like the first Francis in many ways. He had a gentle sweetness about him, but he was not weak or timid. He saw beauty in all things and, like Saint Francis, he had a wealthy father who could afford beauty in all things.

Francis led the life of a well-to-do young man. He had fencing and riding and dancing lessons. He had a private tutor who went with him everywhere, and he learned Latin and Greek and the position of the stars in winter and summer. Francis enjoyed all of this, but most of all he enjoyed being left alone to read the books in the family's library.

It was a large, sunny room with floor-to-ceiling bookshelves covering the walls, ferns and spider plants hanging by the windows and pictures of the family on the mantel. Here Francis would come when the adults were discussing the problems of the world, and he would choose a book, curl up in a deep, soft chair, and lose himself until he was called.

One day it would be a book about Scotland. The next day he would read all about mushrooms. And the next day he would learn about the migration of butterflies or the proper way to make sausages. It was in this way, he said when he was older, he came to know about the world, about goodness and evil, and about finding holiness in all things.

His father encouraged him to read. He felt it would help him in a future career as a lawyer or a diplomat to know a little something about everything. Francis said nothing but continued to read. Already a strong love for God was growing in his heart and he knew he wanted to spend his life working for God. He also knew this did not fit in with his father's plans.

Francis obediently went off to school in Paris when he was fourteen, and then on Padua to study law. He graduated when he was twenty-five, much to his parents' pride. Their son, the lawyer—what a great future lay ahead of him!

One year later Francis told his father he wanted to be a priest. His father was furious. He was the kind of parent who expected his children to obey his wishes without question. Francis did not argue or fight back rebelliously. He was not a thunderstorm person, full of black scowls and sulks. With his patient disposition, he would wait for God to move his father and to wear him down with a rain of grace.

God did just that. Francis became a priest and immediately asked to be sent to a district called Chablais, on the shore of Lake Geneva. This was a rough place where Catholics were not welcome. The people who lived there were called Calvinists and were unfriendly, even violent, toward Catholics.

The Catholics who still lived there were afraid to declare their religion openly and spent most of their time in hiding.

Francis felt that he and his cousin, Louis, were meant to go to them and relight the fire of their faith. They believed they would try to convert their enemies. His father was so upset he went to the bishop to plead that his son not be allowed to go.

"I gave him permission to be a priest, not a martyr!" he said angrily.

Francis was afraid that the bishop would listen to his father. "Would you make me unworthy of the Kingdom of God?" he begged.

The bishop granted Francis permission to go, but Francis' father would not give his son his blessing. Francis and Louis started out on foot to Chablais, and they went directly to the governor's home, which was a fortress, where they would spend their nights.

During the day they went about seeking the hidden Catholics and talking with the natives if they had a hint of friendliness in their eyes. It was a seven-mile walk to the town, a walk filled with all kinds of traps and dangers, robbers, hunters, wild animals and swamps. One night, on his way back to the governor's house, Francis was attacked by wolves. He bolted up the nearest tree and spent the night there (Louis had gone ahead and was safely home).

It was very cold and Francis' hands grew purple and numb from holding tight to the limbs. When daylight came, he was too weak to hold on much longer. Just in time some peasants who were duck hunting found him and got him down. They took him to their cottage and warmed him with food and wine and a good fire. These men were Calvinists, the enemy, without whom Francis might have died. He thanked them with such love and spoke such words of kindness, they were won over, and they became Catholics.

The days and weeks passed into months, and Francis and Louis had little to show for their hard work. They were still chased and cursed and told to go home, but Francis would not lose hope. He remembered his Calvinist rescuers. "We are making but a beginning," he said. "I shall go on in good courage and I hope in God against all human hope."

Francis tried new ways to reach people's hearts. He wrote pamphlets explaining what the church taught and answering charges that were not true. He would slip them under people's doors or give them away at marketplaces or wherever groups of people had gathered. Slowly, more and more people read his words and listened to him. Catholics came back to their faith, and his fame as a gentle persuader spread for miles around Lake Geneva.

His little church was always crowded. Everyone could understand his simple and lively sermons. Never did anyone yawn or fall asleep or even nod when he was speaking. Children sat still and didn't fidget with their shoelaces or pull each other's hair. He talked about things everyone knew— flowers, bees, whiskers, cherries, salt.

Francis said that saints are the salt of the earth, but they must be *in* the earth. They had to live their lives amidst the troubles and joys all people know and prove that being holy means not to do great things but to keep on doing *their* little things, and being patient with others and themselves.

He told his flock to "do all things in the name of God and do all things well, whether you eat or drink, sleep or pray." He spoke of being humble and not puffed up because we think we are something special. (We *are* in God's eyes, but so is everyone else.) He said that "some men become proud because they ride a fine horse, wear a feather in their hat, or are dressed in a fine suit of clothes. How foolish! For if there is any glory in such things, the glory belongs to the horse, the bird and the tailor!"

He reminded us that each of us must use what we have been given. "We are often like those who long for fresh cherries in autumn and for fresh grapes in spring," he said. That is, let us be content with who we are and where we are. "No one should desire to have better talents than he already has."

When he was thirty-two, Francis was made bishop of Geneva, and his father must have been proud of him then! For the next twenty years Francis traveled throughout his diocese, visiting every church, even those at the top of mountains.

He was at home anyplace in the world and said that you could be holy *wherever* you were. He said it was up to us to make what we wanted of ourselves. It didn't matter if we lived in a falling-down house with broken windows and rusty pipes and cockroaches or in a mansion with fresh flowers on the table and a blue telephone and soap in the shape of roses in the bathroom. Of course it might be *harder* if you lived in a mansion, but Francis showed it could be done.

Besides preaching, Francis wrote letters and letters and more letters to people who asked him how to be good and holy. They were filled with such good advice, he put them together in a book which we still read today. He wrote as simply as he spoke, so everyone could understand, yet so elegantly, with every period or comma in its proper place, that the most learned scholars admired his skill.

Francis is the patron saint of writers, and what a help he is when we need him! We can ask him for the patience to write and rewrite and search for just the right word and not give up until we find it, just as he did.

Even his last words before he died have this touch of beauty: "It is toward evening and the day is now far spent." He had spent his day working hard, gathering in his harvest of souls. Now he could rest.

And what an exciting sunrise awaited him!

GERMAINE

Once upon a time in a village in France, there lived a little girl named Germaine. She was born with a crippled hand and a paralyzed arm. She had a disease called scrofula, which was as bad as it sounds. Scabs and runny, messy-looking sores covered her body.

She was very thin and small and pale, and her hair matted into knots that no hairbrush could even untangle. She coughed almost as often as she breathed. On top of everything else, Germaine's body was covered with blue and yellow bruises from her stepmother's beatings.

Little Germaine never knew her real mother. Where Germaine came from, we really don't know. Some say she was the daughter of Laurent Cousin, a wealthy farmer in the town of Pibrac, and a servant girl who worked in his household. Others say she was an orphan left on the Cousin doorstep.

However she got there, nobody cared about her and nobody wanted her, but they allowed her to stay so she could help with chores.

Laurent Cousin's wife took one look at Germaine and shouted, "Out of this house, you ugly little wretch! You make me sick!" She seemed to hate the girl beyond all reason and made her live in the stable, with cows and pigs and sheep and two gray geese. Germaine's bed was a pile of dried vines and straw under the stairs to the hayloft; her blankets were old feedbags. Winter and summer, rain and wind, this was her home.

The stepmother would beat Germaine or kick her, for no reason, until the girl often fell to the ground, senseless. There she would lie in a small, still heap until a curious cow licked her awake. A few times the stepmother threw boiling water over her.

The woman refused to let Germaine come near the kitchen or even to feed her, saying she needed all her scraps for the pigs. Often in the evening, Germaine would creep to the house and look into the kitchen window, watching the heat rise from the stove and smelling the rice pudding and gingerbread and imagining how good warm food must taste.

You might think Germaine had little reason to be happy, and yet, she was. She had been touched by God's grace so early in life that she never doubted God's love for her, no matter what happened. She believed that a beautiful new life awaited her when she had done her best in this one.

Her sheep were her friends. From dawn to sunset, she took them to a nearby forest and tended them, while she talked with God. This was how she spent her days, with daily Mass her only break. Germaine's real joy was going to Mass, and for some reason, her stepmother allowed her to go. When she heard the bells for church, Germaine would stick her staff into the ground and leave the sheep to her guardian angel. Never once did any stray or get eaten by the wolves who were thick in the forest.

People said that little girl had a mysterious power over the wolves, for they never bothered her or her sheep. They would often roar into the village, wild-eyed and hungry, but all Germaine had to do was appear, and they turned as docile as her sheep.

While the sheep grazed, Germaine spun wool. The stepmother was determined that the girl not have one spare moment to waste. Spinning was hard work for Germaine because of her crippled arm, but if she did not have her bundle done by evening, she would be punished.

When she dared to rest from spinning, she made a rosary from a piece of string, painfully knotting each Hail Mary. It was her only possession.

Gradually the villagers began to talk about the holiness of the little girl. At first they too had made fun of her, as the Cousins did, but at heart, they were good people. They saw how she tamed the animals, and, one day in spring, they saw a churning torrent of a stream grow quiet and the waves part to let Germaine pass on her way to church. She walked through without getting even a toe wet.

Another time the villagers saw Germaine's stepmother chasing her down the road, screaming that she was a thief and had better bring back the bread she stole before she got a good beating. The stepmother held a club the size of a baseball bat above her head as she ran. When she caught Germaine, she beat the little girl about the head until she opened her apron and dropped its contents to the ground. Out from it fell not the loaves of bread the stepmother expected to find, but flowers—beautiful, brilliant, fragrant flowers, of a kind never before seen in Pibrac.

The villagers now knew for sure that there was indeed something different about Germaine. They began to treat her with respect, even love. They invited her to eat with them. But their kindness had come too late. Germaine's frail body was too weary even for kindness.

Germaine told God she would live as long as God wanted her to, but at times, oh, how she longed to be warm in heaven with Mary and her real Father, where her body would be healthy, and she could run as fast as the wind.

And God listened and said, "All right, little one," and took her to join the family of heaven. The next morning her sheep "baaa'd," but Germaine did not come out. The Cousins grumbled about the lazy girl and went to get her, and they found Germaine on her pile of straw with the string rosary in her hands.

The night she died, two travelers were lost in the forest where Germaine had tended her sheep. Around midnight, looking to the stars for direction, they saw a wide beam of light like a path from heaven leading to the stable where she had slept. They were frightened, as they watched angels moving down the beam of light. After a few moments, the angels returned, hand in hand with another figure, a little girl with flowers in her hair and circled with light.

To make up for their past unkindnesses to Germaine, the villagers gave her a loving funeral. The ladies of the village wove a garland of carnations and stalks of rye for her hair and placed a white candle in her hands. The stepmother had Germaine's body brought into the house and even bought her a new dress.

Germaine is said to have granted over four hundred miracles (that we know of) to those who asked for her help. Perhaps the miracle she is most pleased with is her stepmother's change of heart.

ROSE OF LIMA

Once there was a girl named Rose who was one of the strangest blooms in God's garden of saints. She was perfectly named—Rose de Flores—for she was as lovely to look at as the most exquisite rose. But she did not yearn to be on exhibit in a crystal vase, to stand tall and elegant and be admired.

Instead she sought to live in the worst soil, hidden in the shade, with her roots cramped. She defied all the rules of proper gardening and yet bloomed joyfully in the midst of thorns and pests.

Rose lived in the country of Peru in the sixteenth century, a time when cruelty and violence were as much a part of life as the hot, humid air. She was born in the city of Lima, to Spanish parents who had come to live in the new land. Spanish soldiers had discovered and conquered Peru and in their greed for gold and land, they had killed the natives who would not accept them as rulers. Those natives who in fear had bowed down to the Spaniards were kept as slaves.

Although most of the fighting had stopped before Rose was born, it still was not a pleasant country to grow up in. Most of the Spanish settlers treated the native slaves kindly, but they did not consider them their equals. Rose and her family did not think much about the troubles of the natives. They had enough of their own problems to settle.

Rose grew up in a large family and, as it is with such a group, there were fights and laughter and feasts and fierce temper explosions. Her mother was a kind woman in quiet moments, but these moments did not come very often. She had a sharp tongue and much on her mind—children growing out of clothes, doctor bills, a job for Rose's father (the tin mine he had begun had closed), and she very much needed a new stove. She suffered and did without for her family, but she did not suffer in silence.

Rose was the peacemaker. She always managed to soothe her mother's ruffled nerves and calm her hot temper. She took care of the other children, played games with them and took them out from under her mother's feet. Often when her mother was upset with one child, Rose would come to the child's rescue and take her away, while her mother's anger fizzled.

Because Rose was so pretty—she had a pink and white complexion, long red curly hair, tiny hands and feet—and charming, her parents dreamed of marrying her to a person of nobility, a duke or a grandee of some sort. Then Rose would not only be settled in a happy life, but also her family would no longer have to worry about money, for it was the custom that a wealthy husband would take care of his wife's family.

So from an early age, Rose was taught to dress and act like a lady. She learned how to sit and how to dance, how to curtsy and how to use her fan. She was sure to chat with older people and offer them the best seats and glasses of lemonade. When she went to parties she wore satin gowns with lace at the bottom, and a chain of gold with a single pearl around her neck, and tortoise shell combs, to hold up her long red hair.

Rose knew she was pretty and that she would soon have to marry, but she was determined she wouldn't. From the time she was a child of six, she had given herself to Christ and promised that everything she did would be for him. She told no one, and on the surface she still seemed a charming butterfly of a girl.

When she finally told her parents of her decision not to marry, there was quite an explosion. This was unheard of! A beautiful girl from a good family—what *else* would she do? Why, half the town's young men would be happy to have her as their bride!

Rose calmly told them nothing would ever change her mind. She knew her family's anger was not only at her "wasted" life, but also at the loss of money that a future husband would bring them.

Rose had worked out in her mind how she could give herself to God and still help her family. She would build a small house in the garden behind their home, and there she would grow flowers and herbs and turn out embroidery and lace to sell. So her parents gave in, but not very happily.

For two years Rose lived in her little sanctuary, working for ten hours, praying for twelve, sleeping for two. She wore an old brown robe day and night. And she grew the loveliest flowers in all of Lima. People stood in line to buy the orchids and gardenias that came from the garden of the strange de Flores girl.

In the afternoon heat, with sweat glistening on her forehead and soaking through her wool robe, Rose embroidered sweet-scented pillows that helped people fall asleep, trying to ignore the mosquitoes that lit on her wet forehead and buzzed in her ears and settled on her ankles.

Rose found the insects hard to bear, and she feared they would bother her enough that she would be tempted to slap and kill them. So she asked them, "Dear little brothers, I know God made you and I love you as I do everything God made. But please could you go somewhere else while I am working? I must do this so my family can live comfortably, and you do distract me when you bite!"

The mosquitoes obediently rose up into one huge choir alongside her. They droned and hummed all afternoon while she worked her needle through the linen. Each day from then on they returned and kept a respectful distance.

Rose often wondered if she should become a nun and live in a real convent. She knew she was not free to do this; still, the desire remained. She asked God for a sign to know what to do. One afternoon, while picking parsley and garlic to sell, a flutter of black and white butterflies flew into the garden. As she watched them, admiring them, they flew above her and formed a rosary in the sky.

Rose's heart leaped up at the sight. She knew what God wanted her to do. They next day she want to the Dominican convent and asked if she might become a member of the Dominican Third Order. She was overjoyed, but not surprised, when they said yes! From that day, she worked in her tiny house wearing the black and white habit of Saint Dominic, satisfied that she was serving both God and her family in the best way she knew.

Rose's gift was very personal and complete—she gave herself. She didn't travel or preach or try to change the wickedness of the world by her protest or reform. She didn't advise kings or bishops or found abbeys. She could have used her beauty and charm in the world to spread God's message, which would have been a normal and practical thing to do. But Rose was neither.

Instead, she chose to use her life as a penance for Christ's suffering for us. He gave her the grace and courage to be different, even a bit odd. The world is full of people who do not look or act or live as we do. If you ask Saint Rose, she will give you the courage not to make fun of people you do not understand. We may not understand them in the least, so we leave them to God, who understands them and loves them. God fashioned them and put his name on their hearts as surely as he did ours.

Let us hope that when Rose reached heaven, she ran joyfully through the fields, with a halo of black and white butterflies hovering about her long red curly hair. And that she *didn't* bring her mosquitoes with her!

JOSEPH OF CUPERTINO

Once upon a time there was a boy named Joseph who was so absentminded he forgot where he was going and why. His mother would pin a note on his shirt with a shopping list, so when people found him wandering around a store, they would know what he was supposed to get.

Joseph forgot to come to meals. He forgot to tie his shoelaces and buttoned his shirt wrong. He forgot the ending of jokes and everyone laughed *at* him instead of *with* him. He never thought of coming in out of the rain.

Things wouldn't have been so bad for Joseph if his parents hadn't expected him to help with chores and be responsible for the tasks they gave him to do. Also, he was thin and sickly and caught every disease that came his way and almost died in his struggle to live. Sometimes they felt that he was just another burden on their weary shoulders.

His teachers didn't think he would ever learn, so his parents took him out of school and apprenticed him to a shoemaker, but he wasn't good at working with his hands either. When Joseph finished a pair of shoes, one foot was always longer than the other, or the sole was put on with the wrong side out, until even the kind shoemaker lost patience.

One day, after Joseph had just smashed his finger with a hammer, a begging friar came into the shop for a bit of leather and tallow and he thought, "I could do that. You don't have to be smart to beg, just smile and say 'Thank you' and run fast if they set the dogs on you. I can do this!"

Joseph asked his family if he could leave to join a monastery. They were so delighted they packed his bag immediately and gave him a salami and an orange for the trip. So Joseph set out for the nearest monastery. The gatekeeper took one look at him, laughed and shut the door quickly. Joseph went to another monastery, and then another with the same result.

But he was determined. He kept going until he found a monastery that took him in as a lay brother, but just on trial. Joseph was very happy and tried his best to remember things and concentrate on what he was doing. But he could see that the monks got fidgety when he was around.

He was especially clumsy in the kitchen, and the other monks called him "Brother Ass." If a bell rang and startled him, he dropped the dishes he was holding and broke them. The prior grumbled, "Soon we shall all have to share our plates if Brother Ass keeps on this way."

Joseph had a way of getting lost in thought about God that made him very unpopular. In the midst of any job, he would suddenly go to his knees, no matter where he was or what he was doing. He might be washing dishes or carrying food or painting the ceiling when he had these "fits" and not even know he had crashed. His brother monks fastened broken bits of dishes onto his habit to warn him not to do this, but it made little difference.

Finally, they told him he must leave. Joseph upset the entire monastery so it was no longer a peaceful place to serve God. The monks took back his habit and gave him some old clothes. He had no hat or shoes or socks, and his coat had seven large holes in it. When he walked through town, the dogs chased the odd-looking stranger and tore the rest of his coat to shreds.

Joseph walked along the road, shivering and unsure where he was going, looking in vain for a friendly smile, or even a friendly dog. Then some shepherds jumped on him, thinking him a dangerous bandit and would have beat him except one of them took pity on him and called the others off.

Joseph continued his travels until he came to a village where one of his uncles lived. How he hoped he would finally be treated kindly and given warm food and clothes! But when his uncle saw him, he was so ashamed to be seen with him that he pushed him away and back into the street.

"You say you are my nephew? You must be out of your mind! No nephew of mine would look and smell as you do!"

In his heart he knew that Joseph was his nephew, but he was too embarrassed to admit it. What would his neighbors think?

Joseph had only one place left to go—home. He arrived hungry, bony, dirty, uglier than ever. He fell at his mother's feet, yearning for her welcoming touch. She pushed him aside with her foot. She was furious that he had returned. Why did he have to make their lives miserable again? She told him to go away—anywhere—and never come back again.

Joseph sat in the road with his head in his hands, wondering why God had put him on this earth. If he was no good to anybody, why was he alive? He wondered if even God cared about him. Then, deep in that part of him that was his soul, he heard God's voice: "Joseph, I will always love you, and Mary loves you. You will always have a mother and father who care deeply about you. Keep your trust in me. I will never let you down, no matter how dark the way seems. Now dry your tears, blow your nose, stand up straight and go right down the road to the Franciscan monastery. There's a stream along the way where you can wash up."

Joseph, with a little bubble of hope in his heart, did as God said. At first, he was refused at the friary, even when he told them God had sent him. Then one of the older friars said, "Wait, let's give him a chance. It *may* be that God willed him to come here."

They found work for him in the stable taking care of the friary mule. Joseph laughed and thought, "At last there is a place for Brother Ass!"

Joseph had much time to think in the stable. Nobody rushed him for an answer or gave him jobs he couldn't do. And he was content. If he was to be a servant to animals, very well. If that was all he was fit for, he vowed, he would be the best mule-tender on God's earth. He asked for nothing. He took what was given in the way of food and clothes and slept on a plank of wood in the stable.

The friars would shake their heads and wonder what that crazy Joseph was up to *now*, but they would find reasons to go to the stable and check up on him and share some of his happiness. The villagers outside the monastery were also drawn to the stable where the lighthearted little man welcomed everyone. His holiness touched their hearts, right up to the superior of the monastery.

The superior wondered if Joseph would be able to study for the priesthood. Everyone else thought that might be asking too much of both Joseph and God. But by a miracle, this impossible dream came true. At the age of twenty-five, Joseph was ordained a priest. Brother Ass had proved that nothing is impossible for those who love God!

But his holiness was still the cause of angry explosions among the friars. It was a habit which Joseph could not control, and he himself would become upset when he realized the commotion he had created. Often he would lose himself in thinking about God and rise straight up into the air. This happened most often in church, when he would circle around the altar and up to the ceiling where he would hover until Mass was over, but it could happen anywhere.

Sometimes he would rise during mealtime when he would be listening to a holy reading and become so absorbed that he would go straight up with his bowl of soup in his hands. This would distract his brother friars greatly. It is not a comfortable feeling to have someone flying overhead with a bowl of hot soup in his hands.

Sometimes it came upon him when he was outdoors, and he would fly up into the branches of a tree and contemplate the beauty of everything. It took little to set Joseph in motion—a hymn to Mary, the velvet sheen of a plum, a crimson sunrise, and off he would soar into the sky.

His love went out to the animals and birds too, and they returned it. Once when Joseph came to offer Mass for harvest workers in a chapel in the field, he found everyone but the sheep he had left. So he said, "Dear sheep, it's just us tonight. Come, let us honor Mary, our mother, who loves you too." The sheep came running, leaping over bushes and gathering around Joseph, anxious to be his congregation. He knelt down and began the litany of Mary's name, and sheep answered every one with a reverent *"Baaaaaaa."*

Joseph began to work miracles other than making hearts happy. He touched the eyes of a blind boy, and the boy saw. He held the hand of a dying child and the child was cured, leaping up and asking for his supper. As is sometimes the way, some people became jealous of Joseph's gift and told lies about him and said he was really evil.

He was called before the pope to explain his strange ways. Joseph had not thought his ways strange; everything he had done, he had done for the love of God. He had just wanted to be a very good mule-tender, and the rest just *happened*.

The pope decided that Joseph could not go back to the friary. Instead Joseph was to go to one hidden far away in the hills where no one would ever find him. At first Joseph was very sad, because he had come to love that place, but then he thought of how much our Lord had given up for him. Now Joseph could pay him back.

The same wonderful things happened to him in the new friary. He would kneel to pray while in the garden and then rise to the tops of the rose bushes to pick a bouquet for our Lady. Joseph died there when he was sixty years old, with a smile on his face that looked as if he had just heard the best joke ever and couldn't wait to pass it on.

KATERI TEKAKWITHA

Once upon a time there was a girl named Tekakwitha whose family was among the very first settlers of our country. No, she didn't come over on the *Mayflower*, or on a Viking or French or Spanish boat before that. She was already here before the pale-skinned people set foot. She was a Native American.

Tekakwitha was born to an Algonquin native named Kehenta, who had been captured by the Mohawks, members of the Iroquois nation. The mother's life had been spared because the Mohawks' chief had fallen in love with her and decided she would be his wife. Kehenta did not want to marry him, but she knew she had no choice. She knew she was alive only through his mercy; to say "No" to him would not only be rude, it would be foolish.

Kehenta had been baptized a Christian by the Blackrobes, the native's name for the French priests who had come from across the sea to tell them about the Great Spirit, Manitou, and his Son. Kehenta prayed that if she had children, they too would be sprinkled with the "blessed water," but she dared not speak of such things to her warrior husband who felt no love toward the French.

In a few years, she did have a daughter and a son, and as she watched them playing hide-and-seek in the bushes, she would dream of the time when the whole family would come to know her God as she did. But she kept these hopes quietly in her heart. When the time was right, it would happen.

Kehenta had other things to fill her mind. Always there were surprise attacks from other natives who were enemies. There was the dreaded smallpox fever that was spreading throughout the Iroquois nation. Every family had lost a dear one and the sounds of moaning and weeping came from every tent. Kehenta and her husband and son were among those who died. Only little Tekakwitha was left. Then she too caught the smallpox and lay ill for weeks, as ashen and still as if she were already dead.

But her mother's old friend, Anastasia, stayed day and night and nursed the little girl back to health. It wasn't really *health*; it was more the desire to sit up and stand up, to finally move around and feel the sun again.

Tekakwitha was only four years old, and the sickness had left its mark on her. Her face, once so bright and brown and shining, was now full of ugly pockmarks, her skin dry and wrinkled. And she could no longer see all those beautiful sights which brought joy to her heart. Her eyes were so weak that that she had to wear a shade bonnet to protect them from the sun. Everything she saw was blurry, fuzzy and rippled.

Tekakwitha went to live with Anastasia, who loved the girl as if she were her granddaughter. Anastasia told Tekakwitha stories of Jesus, the Son of the Great Spirit, who had come to save the world and everyone in it, even their enemies. She taught Tekakwitha the Sign of the Cross and the rosary. When Tekakwitha's uncle, now the chief, saw this, he became furious.

He accused Anastasia of casting spells when she made the Sign of the Cross. It would bring the demons down upon them, he said. He would hear no more about this God of the Blackrobes. "The God of the white man has done nothing for us but bring ruin to our lives. They take our land and our traps and burn our lodges and poison us with their firewater! Why should we worship their God?"

He took Tekakwitha to live with him and his glum-faced wife who was not happy to have another mouth to feed. Besides, this child couldn't see beyond her nose. She'd be no good for planting beans or squash, but she could get water and grind corn. So Tekakwitha said a sad goodbye to Anastasia, who whispered to her not to forget her mother and the Great Spirit. They would keep her from being lonely.

The young girl was just beginning to get used to her new home when scouts arrived at the camp warning of an attack by the French, the Hurons and the Algonquins. They were gathering to destroy the Mohawk camp. Tekakwitha shuddered to think of all the killing and torture to come. Both the Iroquois and French were very cruel. Each side did terrible things because the *other* side did it. Neither side would stop first.

The Blackrobes traveled with the French, not because they were a part of the army, but because they knew they could be of comfort to the wounded and dying, whether French or native. The priests' first purpose was to teach the natives about God, at any opportunity. Tekakwitha longed to meet a Blackrobe and to learn all she could about her mother's *Jezos*.

She had her chance the next spring. After a winter filled with surprise attacks, burning of lodges, running, hiding, rebuilding and starting all over again, the chiefs of the

Iroquois nation signed a peace treaty with the French. For the first time in Tekakwitha's life, she would go to sleep at night without the sound of war drums coming into her dreams and waking her.

One fine spring morning, three Blackrobes arrived by canoe to visit for three days. Tekakwitha was very excited. Not one but three! Then she feared for them. How would her uncle receive them? Would he torture them as he had vowed he would?

He did not. He dared not touch them because it had been part of the treaty that the Blackrobes be permitted to travel among the tribes. So her uncle, though calm and aloof, was polite. He offered them the hospitality of the village, and they sat together in a circle with the council members, smoking the pipe of peace.

Tekakwitha listened eagerly to what the Blackrobes told her people. They talked of the Son of the Great Spirit, who loved the wind and sun and earth and called the birds and animals his brothers. They told stories of the saints, the holy ones who had done great deeds for the Great Spirit, and of Mary, the mother of Jezos. They spoke of heaven and how we must often suffer with patience the happenings in our lives that lead us there. Tekakwitha tucked all this into her memory so she could think about these things as she lay under the buffalo robes at night.

When Tekakwitha was sixteen, her aunt and uncle decided it was time for her to marry. She knew they would choose the bravest, strongest Mohawk warrior as would befit the daughter of a chief.

"It won't be easy," sighed her aunt. "She's not at all pretty and has those awful pockmarks on her face. Still, she does have pleasant brown eyes, and she works hard at whatever she does. She would make a worthwhile, helpful squaw."

Tekakwitha did not want to marry a Mohawk brave or any

brave. She wanted, first of all, to become a Christian, and she didn't want to marry anybody. It was unheard of that a native girl refuse to marry. She knew she must tell her uncle soon because he was already making arrangements. Tekakwitha finally got up enough courage to speak to her uncle one night as he sat smoking his pipe.

"My uncle," she said, her voice shaking a bit, "please don't ask me to marry. I cannot. I *will not*. I love and respect you very much but I cannot obey you in this. Please don't force me!"

Her uncle was just as angry as she thought he would be, and her aunt threw up her hands and said, "Listen to her, that ungrateful girl! Those Blackrobes must have filled her head with this nonsense."

Together they decided that they would have to trick her into marriage. One evening they told her to put on her finest robes and braid her hair with scarlet beads because they were having a special guest for supper. When the guests came, they went immediately to her uncle and each one presented him with a gift. Tekakwitha was seated next to a handsome brave, and her aunt bade her offer him a bowl of corn.

She was about to do this when she remembered that this was a part of the Mohawk marriage ceremony. When a young woman presented the bowl to a brave in the presence of their families and he accepted it, it meant that they were married.

Tekakwitha was so upset she dropped the bowl and ran out of the house into the dark woods. You can imagine how angry her aunt and uncle were, and how she feared coming home, as she knew she must. When she finally returned, she begged their pardon for her rude behavior. They treated her coldly and acted as if she weren't even there.

The next few months were miserable for Tekakwitha. No one spoke to her, except to give her orders, because she had disgraced the entire tribe. She worked alone and silently in the fields, dreaming of the day she might join Christian friends in another settlement. She wondered how it would be to pray to Jezos openly and with others who felt as she did. It would take a miracle to get her out of here, and that's what she prayed for.

One day, when she was hoeing the melons, she felt a sharp, stabbing pain in her foot. She looked down and saw blood spurting from it. She had chopped her toe with her hoe. When she saw it, she got very dizzy. The women carried her to her tent, her aunt all the while muttering about the lazy girl who would do anything to get out of work.

The pain was getting worse; her whole foot throbbed and turned red. Tekakwitha heard a soft step and saw the shadow of a Blackrobe passing by her tent. Quickly she called to him. He came in and saw her wound, cleaned it with water, and wrapped it with herbs and a clean cloth to keep the dirt out. As he worked, Tekakwitha told him her story, at first timidly, then with growing trust that this white man could help her. And then she asked to be baptized a Christian.

The Blackrobe, whose name was Father de Lamberville, told Tekakwitha what she was not happy to hear—that she must tell her uncle of her desire. She must not be frightened, no matter how ferocious he might become. He would not hurt her, the priest said, because he wanted no trouble with the French.

With her heart thumping, she went again to her uncle to tell him something that would not please him. To her surprise, he said wearily, almost sadly, "You may do as you wish. Perhaps you will be happier as a Christian than as a Mohawk. You certainly aren't happy now." She hurried to Father de Lamberville with the incredible news, and on Easter morning, she was baptized Catherine (*Kateri* in her language) Tekakwitha.

Now that she was a Christian, the tribe did worse than ignore her. They laughed at her and pushed her and threw stones as she tried to go about her work. The Blackrobe felt it would be safer for her if she left the Mohawks to live in a Christian Native American village in Canada, which they could reach by traveling the St. Lawrence River. They would have to plan her escape carefully and secretly. If her uncle ever found out she wanted to leave, he might scalp her himself.

Kateri believed that God would show her the way to escape and the right time. It came seven months later, with the arrival in the village of three Christian Native Americans. One of them was named Hot Ashes, because of his quick temper and wit. It was arranged that she would leave with them before dawn, and the sun would be high before she was missed.

At the cry of an owl, which was really the native's signal to begin the escape, Kateri crept out of her tent and ran lightly to join the others waiting in the bushes. They ran quickly, without speaking, to the waiting canoes and paddled many miles before they were visible in the early morning sun.

They left the canoes and hid them and took to the forest trail. Then they heard the sounds of twigs snapping behind them and heavy-footed steps growing ever closer. It was her uncle! He was determined to find Kateri and bring her home to her village. "Quick, Kateri," whispered Hot Ashes, "go with the Huron. Your uncle is almost upon us. I will stand here and pretend to be hunting. It is too late to try and hide. Now go quickly!"

The panting chief reached him, and Hot Ashes pretended not to see him. He shot an arrow into a tree, as if he had just seen a porcupine in its limbs. The chief ran right past, as if Hot Ashes were of no importance.

Kateri was ready to drop, she was so tired from running. The Huron motioned to her to lie down. He covered her with twigs and leaves and moss and then sat on her, smoking his pipe. His eyes were closed, as if he were thinking deep thoughts. The chief stopped and looked at him closely through his sweating eyelids. "Have you seen Tekakwitha?" he wheezed.

"Who?" asked the Huron, pretending to be innocent.

"Tekakwitha! My niece—a small girl, face full of scars. Have you seen her?"

The Huron frowned. "Girl? I've seen no girl." He shook his head and puffed once more on his pipe.

The chief looked at him in disgust. "Bah! Those dumb Hurons, no wonder so many of them have become Christians! Well," he sighed bitterly, "if that is how she wants it, then I shall let her go. Let the animals and the Blackrobes have her. She'll be sorry she didn't stay with her own kind."

As soon as he was certain Kateri's uncle had really gone, the Huron stood up quickly and brushed the leaves and twigs off the little girl. "Have I flattened you, Kateri? Breathe deep, you'll fill up again. At least you're still alive—and *free*! Did you hear?"

With the help of her Native American friends, Kateri soon reached the community called Praying Castle, where she would spend the rest of her life. Her new friends welcomed her, as well as one dear old one—Anastasia. Although Anastasia was more wrinkled and moved slower than when Kateri had first learned the Sign of the Cross from her, they knew each other instantly. The old woman hugged Kateri as if she would never let her go. How happy Kateri's mother must be in heaven, Anastasia thought, knowing that her daughter was now a Christian!

Kateri at last knew the love she had sought all her life. She began each day with Mass and then spent the rest of it wherever she was needed. She worked in the fields and nursed the sick and taught the children songs and games about God and Jezos.

When she was twenty-four years old, Kateri and her frail body were ready to return to heaven. Since her favorite season was spring, she left her life here at just the right time, Wednesday of Holy Week, to spend Easter in heaven. To those friends who clung about her bed, she gave a happy sign of her new life. A few moments after she had died, the Blackrobe took one last look at Kateri and his eyes opened wide in amazement.

"Look," he cried, "look, everyone, at Kateri's face!"

Everyone saw the lovely, brown, shining, smooth face of a healthy young girl. No scars, no wrinkles, no ugly little holes. They were all gone, along with the sufferings of her old life. How wonderful it must have been to see the wonders of heaven with eyes as sparkling-sharp as crystal!

JUNIPERO SERRA

There are some saints who seem to be full-blown and brimming with God's grace. They know from childhood what they will do in this life and plow ahead determinedly to do it. These are most often the missionaries who must spread the good news to the farthest, most obscure corners of the world, missionaries such as Francis Xavier, Frances Cabrini, Mother Teresa and—Junipero Serra.

Junipero was born Miguel Jose Serra on November 24, 1713, on the island of Majorca, off Spain. His parents, who owned a farm, reared him lovingly, and he seems to have had a comfortable, uneventful life with them. He had the Majorcan love of beauty and spent hours watching the clouds and listening to the music of the sea, dreaming of how it might be someday to travel to faraway lands.

When he was seventeen years old, he joined the Franciscans, hoping that when he was a priest, he would be sent as missionary to New Spain, which is what the Spanish colonies in South and Central America and Mexico were called.

At ordination he took the name of Junipero, in honor of Saint Francis' high-spirited companion. Still on fire to convert "the heathen," he immediately put in a request to sail with the next expedition. But his superiors had other ideas. They wanted to keep his brilliant mind—even at his young age, he was a noted preacher and professor of philosophy—at the university. They did not want to "waste" him by sending him off to the natives.

But he persevered for eighteen years and finally, at the age of thirty-six, he was given permission to sail with the next expedition. With him would go his former pupil and dear friend, Francisco Palou, and nineteen other friars. The mission was not only to convert souls but also to explore and claim the unknown lands above Mexico known as Alta California, "to extend the dominion of the king...and to protect California from the ambitious projects of foreign nations."

Spain was very worried that England and Russia, who were also sending ships for the same purpose, might get to California before they did, so that might have been the most important push for the expedition. Junipero didn't care, he was going! His joy was mixed with sadness, for he knew he would never again see his parents or this beloved land of sheep-dotted hills and Castilian roses. But he knew that this was why he had come to earth, and that God would give him and his parents the courage to say good-bye.

And so, on August 28, 1749, Junipero and Francisco and the other friars set sail from Cadiz, Spain, to begin their journey across the Atlantic. By November, the boat, battered and broken by storms, with its weary and sick passengers, made its way into the harbor of Vera Cruz, Mexico.

So many of the friars were weakened by hunger that they

stayed behind to recuperate while Junipero and one young friar decided to walk to Mexico City. If walking was good enough for Saint Francis, said Junipero, surely it was good enough for him!

But he soon realized he had not made a wise decision, for he did not know the geography of this country or the dangers that lurked behind the thick jungle of trees and vines. Yet always when they were in need of help, it came. Once when they were stopped by a deep river and didn't know how they would cross, a voice called, telling them to walk along the bank and they did, until the voice guided them to a shallow place where they could cross easily.

Once when they were thirsty, a stranger appeared, saying nothing, and gave them pomegranates, and another time, when their stomachs growled with hunger, someone came and brought each a loaf of bread. Junipero never doubted that these strangers were angels, or even Saint Joseph, come to help them.

They were almost to Mexico City, when Junipero felt a sudden, sharp pain in his leg. He cried out and looked down to see a snake slithering away into the undergrowth. He refused to give the bite any attention. "It is nothing," he said. "It will be better by morning."

But it wasn't. By morning the leg was red and swollen, and the open sore where the snake had bit him began to ooze with infection. He could barely put his weight on it. A muleteer whom they encountered put an ointment of herbs and hot wax, a treatment he used for the animals, on Junipero's leg, and that helped cleanse it and eased the pain temporarily. But it never healed completely. For the rest of his life Junipero walked with a limp, with pain as his constant companion.

When they arrived in Mexico City, a great fuss was made over him, for his fame as a preacher was known even there. "Oh that I had a forest of junipers like that this one!" the college rector exclaimed in his eager welcome. Gifts and invitations to dinner besieged him, and Junipero began to worry. He had not crossed the Atlantic to minister to the rich and live a comfortable, privileged life as a cathedral preacher. He wanted to be with his chosen people, the Native Americans, living with them, baptizing, teaching and fighting for them.

Finally he was permitted to set up a mission in Lower California, the Baha peninsula, for the Pamé Native Americans of the Sierra Gorde. He would still, now and then, be summoned to preach at the cathedral, but this was a minor inconvenience to Junipero.

At the mission, he learned the native language and was able to translate prayers, hymns and the catechism into it. Nothing was too much trouble for the people he called his "beloved children," and they responded to his love. Junipero taught these hunters and gatherers how to improve the soil and plant and grow their own food. He taught the older men how to make bricks and tiles, and the younger ones learned carpentry and tanning and blacksmithing. He gave the women looms so they could weave their own clothes, something they delighted in.

Junipero and Francisco often left the mission to find other members of the Pamé people, traveling over two thousand miles through the wildest parts of Mexico. Once they went up the Migres River in a canoe and came upon sharks in the deep parts of the river. Poisonous snakes hissed at them from the bank, the puma and jaguar in the brush growled low at the foolish humans, and all the while, they were followed by clouds of mosquitoes.

When friends tried to dissuade him from these trips—suppose another snake might bite him, what then?—Junipero just smiled and said, "I am on the Lord's business. God can take care of me and the business too."

On one of these journeys, when they were quite tired and night was falling, they came upon a small house in a clearing. It was Spanish style, not native as they might have expected. An elderly man came out, then a lovely young woman holding a child. They were neither native or Spanish. The family welcomed Junipero and Francisco to their home, gave them a good, simple meal and a place to sleep. In the morning they said their goodbyes, and the friars blessed the family for their kindness.

When Junipero got back to the mission, he could not get the couple out of his mind. He asked everyone about them, describing them and the house and the cottonwood trees around it, but no one knew of any such people or house. Junipero and several other friars went back to the spot, but the house was not there. The cottonwood trees and thorn bushes were there—but nothing else.

Junipero understood. He knelt in the sandy earth and realized that they had been granted heavenly hospitality. "God be thanked," he cried. "God has shown us the house of Nazareth and granted us a vision of the Holy Family!"

For eighteen years Junipero worked in the Baja peninsula. Then, because the English and Russian threat grew stronger, the Viceroy of Mexico decided to send a large force into Alta (Upper) California consisting of four expeditions, two by land and two by sea. Each expedition had both soldiers and friars. The commanding officer of Junipero's expedition, Gaspar de Portola, did not want Junipero to come because his lameness would slow down the pace. Yet he admitted that Junipero "understands the Indian; he is courageous and resourceful, he faced hardship with a gay heart...." So he reluctantly accepted him.

And so *Commandante* Portola and *Presidente* (of the missions) Serra began their trek of exploring and transforming what we now call the state of California. For the next thirteen years, they preserved, plodded, cut paths through forest and flowering fields, stumbled over rocky slopes, scaled mountains, thirsted over deserts, ran out of supplies and food, fought off native attacks, disease and rebellions within their own groups.

The soldiers and the friars were often at odds over how to treat the natives. To the soldiers, the natives were of no importance other than slaves; they were not considered equals. To the friars, the natives' souls were of first importance, yet their rights and equal treatment in the world were also considered. When the missions were founded, Junipero made sure they were built away from the barracks, so the soldiers could not frighten or take advantage of the new Christians.

Along the way to San Diego, the first mission claimed for Spain, the friars blazed a trail that would become known as *El Camino Real*—the King's Highway. They did not use the usual trees or stones, which might be destroyed by the natives, but wild mustard seed. Junipero scratched a line alongside the path beaten down by men and animals and scattered a handful of the tiny black seeds onto it.

"The King's Highway must be bordered with gold," he said. "In springtime and summer, these plants will show us where we walked and will guide our way." The soldiers ran for hoes and helped him plant the seeds. Even the *Commandante* grudgingly approved. "One of your better ideas, Father Serra. *El Camino Real*—a good name!"

They continued on, for thousands of miles, and in the years between 1769 and 1782, Junipero established nine missions: San Diego, San Juan Capistrano, San Gabriel, San Luis Obispo, San Antonio de Padua, San Carlos Borromeo, Santa Clara, San Francisco and San Buenaventura. Twelve more were founded after his death.

Some say the friars enslaved the natives as much as the soldiers by forcing them into Christianity. There are others who feel differently, such as Agnes Repplier, in her book *Junipero Serra*. She quotes Alexander Forbes, who wrote a history of California in 1835, and who detested religion in general and priests in particular, yet said:

> Considering the absolute authority possessed by the missionaries, their conduct has been marked by a degree of humanity, moderation, and benevolence unexampled in any other situation. There were few instances to be found where men, enjoying such...confidence and power, have not abused them....Yet the missionaries of California neither betray their trust nor show themselves unworthy of confidence....Since the country has been opened up, strangers have found in their missions disinterested hospitality and kindness.

Junipero died at the age of seventy-one at the mission of San Carlos, with his dear friend, Francisco Palou, beside him. When the bells tolled the news that "the old father" had died, the natives came running, crying, bringing armfuls of the wildflowers he loved and heaped them about him.

At his funeral, the cannons boomed in salute, the bells rang in celebration, and Junipero, set free, strode joyfully and without limp, up to the King's Highway bordered with *real* gold!

BENEDICT JOSEPH LABRE

There's an old proverb that says "Cleanliness is next to godliness." If that is the case, you would think saints would be the cleanest people on earth. Many of them were, but this is the story of Benedict Joseph Labre, who wasn't. He was dirty, he did not bathe (although he once jumped into a river to save a child), and he did not wash his clothes. And he smelled bad. *Very* bad.

He didn't start out that way. He was born to good, clean, loving parents in the town of Amette, France, in 1748. The eldest of fourteen children, he was a gentle child, cheerful with a touch of sadness, who took life seriously. He was not mischievous or lighthearted, but he wasn't sour or priggish either.

He would often visit his uncle, a priest in a nearby village, and read the books in his library about penance and hell and damnation. Benedict decided he would spend his life away from the world and its comforts and pleasure. He would enter a Trappist monastery and be safe from temptations. Here he would be able to deny himself completely for Christ.

He went first to a Carthusian monastery, where he was turned down, and then on to another, where he was at first accepted and then asked to leave because he was found not suitable for community life. He went on to a Trappist monastery, only to be rejected again. Sadly he returned home to work and pray for a year, until he had the grace and courage to try again.

Over and over he was accepted, then rejected, seven times altogether. Desolate, dejected, he wondered what he would do next. He would not return home. Gradually it began to dawn on him that his vocation was not in joining a monastery, that he was stubbornly trying to serve God in *his* way instead of God's.

Very well then, he decided, if he could not be a monk in a monastery, he would follow the example of our Lord and stay in the world. The world would be his cloister. He would travel the dusty roads, "carrying neither purse, nor scrip, nor provisions for the way." He would be a tramp, an outcast, God's poor man, in the company of other beggars, thieves, the unwanted and despised. He would depend upon the kindness of strangers for food and money; if no kind strangers came his way, he would poke among the garbage heaps for crusts of bread and wilted vegetables.

So, at the age of twenty-five, he began walking. He wore a long, tattered cloak with a rope around his waist, a rosary around his neck, a sack slung over his shoulder to hold a few prayer books and a cracked wooden bowl, and ripped, torn shoes "with more uppers than soles." He became one of the homeless poor, sleeping on the ground at night, enduring beatings and misunderstandings.

He was once thrown out of a church as a suspected thief, and into jail for trying to help a man beaten by robbers. He had ripped a piece from his cloak and soaked it in a stream and was washing the man's wounds when he was dragged off mistakenly as one of the robbers. Inside the prison, he as usual made no complaint and began singing our Lady's litany to beg for coins from passersby who could see the prisoners through the bars. When he was identified as the man's rescuer and friend, he gave all the money he collected to the other prisoners.

For seven years his pilgrimages led him through France, Italy, Germany and Spain. You can imagine that traveling in the same clothes, winter and summer, Benedict became unpleasantly smelly. We may wonder why he didn't bathe. You would think a saint would be sensitive about offending others, but Benedict's only concern was that he not offend our Lord. What people thought of him was not important.

Still, it must have been hard for him, because he didn't set out to be repulsive. It just worked out that way, and he accepted it as part of his sacrifice. He knew that the sense of smell touches the emotions more quickly than the gifts of sight and hearing. The fragrance of roses or gingerbread baking in the oven or your mother's perfume are delightful comforts, while the odors of stinking fish, rotten cabbage or spoiled eggs can make us bad-tempered and mean. (Hell must be a place of never-ending bad smells.)

But despite the smell and the rags and the lice that lived on him (he would not send them to vermin heaven because he felt even the most loathsome creatures had a right to live), people were drawn to him and followed him and asked his advice. This bothered him, because he felt himself unworthy of any such attention, but he never turned away from them.

There were many stories of his healing incurable invalids and multiplying food for the hungry, and even though there was no radio or television to report his doings, word soon spread about The Holy Beggar, The Hermit of the Road and, yes, The Great Unwashed. It seems he couldn't contain his holiness any more than he could the lice.

Weary and weak from his travels, he decided to stay in Rome, as always spending his days in church and his nights in the ruins of the Coliseum. His poor body was so worn out, he finally accepted the offer of friends to live in a hospice with twelve other homeless men. Despite the fact that for the first time in years he had a place to sleep and enough food to eat, he caught a chill and a cough that quickly worsened.

On Wednesday of Holy Week, he fainted on the steps of a church. A butcher who knew him and who lived nearby carried him into his home. Benedict, old at the age of thirty-five, died there that evening, just as the bells began ringing their daily *Salve Regina*. Immediately, in all parts of Rome, children began the cry, "The saint is dead! The saint is dead!" and then everybody took it up, with the bells still chiming. It was as if the bells were proclaiming the glorious news that the saint of the poor and the lonely wanderers had arrived at his destination.

Can you imagine how much he must have enjoyed that warm, heavenly bubble bath before putting on his clean Easter robes?

PIERRE TOUSSAINT

The exciting thing about saints is that you never know where they will pop up or what they'll be doing. It doesn't surprise us when they're kings or queens, teachers or writers or doctors. We almost expect them to be doing something noble. But every now and then we find a holy one wrapped in the guise of beggar or dishwasher or juggler or some other way of life we might take for granted. Did you ever consider that your mail carrier could be a saint? Or the person who cuts your hair?

That is the story of Pierre Toussaint, who was a hairdresser and is now a saint. Pierre was born a slave on the island of San Domingue, which is now called Haiti. In 1776 it was a lush, lovely land governed by planters who had come from France to make their fortune raising sugar cane. They lived luxurious lives on their plantations, while their slaves worked in the fields and as servants in their houses.

Pierre and his family belonged to the Berards who, unlike many owners, treated their slaves with kindness and respect, taught them to read and write, and made them as comfortable as possible. Their slaves returned their affection. But the other planters had no such regard for the human beings they considered their inferiors. They forced the slaves to work long hours in the sun and beat them when they fell exhausted from the heat. The angry slaves planned secretly to rebel and overthrow their masters, and, if need be, kill them to gain freedom.

Monsieur Jean Berard, newly married, feared that San Domingue would soon be a bloody battlefield, so he decided to move his wife, Marie, and her sisters, along with Pierre and his sister, Rosalie, to New York City, the capital of the brand new country called the United States of America.

He apprenticed Pierre to a hairdresser in the city to learn the trade and also to be on hand to take care of the women of the household. Hairstyles then weren't at all like ours today. For one thing, there wasn't the choice between short and bouncy or long and curly. Styles were as fancy as a three-tier wedding cake. So a personal hairdresser was a very necessary part of a wealthy, elegant lady's life.

Pierre became so skillful at his work that he attracted many society women who attended the Berard parties, and his days were soon filled with appointments. Everyone wanted "Toussaint," as they called him, for he was more than hairdresser to them, he was their friend. They shared their problems and anxieties with this gentle man who was always willing to listen. He advised them, never judged them and never carried gossip from one salon to another. All secrets stayed in his heart.

The revolution in Haiti proved to be as bloody as Monsieur Berard had feared. Madame Berard grew sad and homesick.

She worried about her husband, who had returned to check on their plantation. After months of waiting, she received word that he had died of a fever and that their beautiful home had been burned. Now everything and everyone was gone from her once happy life. She had nothing.

Pierre immediately took over. With his own money, he paid the bills for the household, bought the food and brought little treats of candy and flowers to try to cheer Madame Berard. He never allowed anyone outside the family to know, for he felt it would not do for the world to know that a slave was supporting his mistress.

When she met a young musician and married him, Pierre hoped her life would be happy. Then his sister Rosalie married, but her husband left her when she was expecting a baby. Pierre took on his growing family without complaint.

He worked all the harder, beginning each day with 6 A.M. Mass, then walking to all his appointments. Because he was black, he was not allowed to ride the horesecars. This must have hurt him, but as always, his cheerful manner and lively step made it appear that all was well with his world.

Madame Berard's marriage failed and she grew ill in body and spirit. She was anxious to leave this world, but before she died, she granted Pierre his freedom. Finally, at the age of forty-one, he was no longer a slave. He was a free man!

He married Juliette Noel, a refugee from Haiti, and they adopted his niece, Euphemia (Rosalie had died soon after her baby was born). They had an instant, loving family.

Euphemia was the delight of his life, a joyful, pretty child. He would carry her astride his shoulders on walks, and often took her on his rounds of appointments. Pierre beamed with pleasure when the ladies fussed over her. No father ever loved a daughter more.

When she died at the age of fourteen from tuberculosis, the sadness almost crushed Pierre's heart, but slowly, with Juliette's help, he resumed his life. He knew there were other children, the orphans and widows, the sick and lonely, who needed the help he could give, so he worked even harder and longer.

He was proud of his race, and he and Juliette were benefactors of St. Vincent de Paul School, the first New York City school for black children. They also helped support the Oblate Sisters of Providence, a religious order of black women in Baltimore. But he was not one to publicly protest or reform the unfair status of slaves. Only once, in response to the violence suggested to solve the slavery problem, did he comment: "They have not seen what I have seen...." The memories of the bloodshed in Haiti would always be painful for him.

Pierre grew to old age, his lively step slowed down, and he did not stand as tall as he once did. Still, he worked.

"Pierre," asked a friend, "you are the richest man I know. Why don't you stop working?"

"Then, Madame," he said, "I should not have enough for others." And he always had "enough."

Pierre died at the age of eighty-seven and was buried beside Juliette and Euphemia in Old St. Patrick's Cemetery on Mott Street in New York City. The famous Revolutionary War general Philip Schuyler said about Pierre: "I have known Christians who were not gentlemen, gentlemen who were not Christians. One man I know who is both and that man is black." And his name was Pierre Toussaint.

ROSE PHILIPPINE DUCHESNE

When Rose Philippine Duchesne was a little girl living in Grenoble, France, she declared that when she was old enough, she would go to the New World (the United States) to teach the Native Americans about God. Her parents smiled and paid no attention. They thought she had been listening to too many tales brought back to France by Jesuit missionaries. Her father, a lawyer and politician, and her mother, a social worker, had a different life planned for her.

But Philippine (although she was baptized Rose, she seems to have dropped the name in childhood) was a stubborn child. As she grew older, she evolved into a fiercely independent, strong-willed young woman. When she decided to do something, Philippine was like a steamroller and everyone got out of her way. In 1788, at the age of eighteen, she entered the convent of the Visitation nuns in Grenoble, without asking her parents' permission or even telling them. They were quite upset, to put it mildly. Their plans for her included a suitable marriage with a socially acceptable husband, but Philippine would have none of it. She *would* be a missionary in the New World, and that was that.

Meanwhile, in the world outside the convent, the French Revolution had erupted and thrown the country into bloody upheaval. Monasteries and convents were closed down and their occupants absorbed back into their families as laypeople. For ten years, Philippine worked in her community teaching the children, visiting the sick and imprisoned, and secretly giving sanctuary to outlawed priests.

Eventually the "Reign of Terror" ended with the Concordat of 1804, and Philippine tried to resurrect her convent at Grenoble. But she could find only four of her sister nuns who would return, and both the spirit and funds to rebuild were lacking. So at the invitation of Mother Sophie Barat, founder of the newly formed Society of the Sacred Heart, Philippine and her friends joined that order.

Mother Sophie was the Superior General and would also become Philippine's lifelong friend and one of the anchors in her life. There was always honesty between them, and a delicate diplomacy on Mother Sophie's part in respecting Philippine's temperament. After she made her final vows in 1805, Philippine confided her old urging to her Superior General. She told her of an experience she had during her adoration of the Holy Eucharist on Holy Thursday: "I spent the entire night in the New World…carrying the Blessed Sacrament to all parts of the land….I had all my sacrifices to offer: mother, sisters, family, my mountain! When you say to me 'now I send you,' I will respond quickly, 'I go!'"

Philippine had to wait another twelve years, but finally the opportunity came. The bishop of New Orleans had requested Mother Sophie to send teachers for the French and Native

American children of the diocese, and so, at the age of forty-nine, Philippine, with four other nuns, was on her way to the New World. As she boarded the ship and waved goodbye to her family, community and dear Mother Sophie, the sadness of knowing she probably would never see them again was mixed with the exhilaration of the fulfillment of her dream.

When they arrived in New Orleans, after eleven weeks at sea, they found that the bishop had no place for them to work or live, so he sent them up the Mississippi to the town of St. Charles, Missouri, which Philippine called "the remotest village in the U.S." Here the colony of five lived in a small log cabin in the woods and eventually built the first free school west of the Mississippi.

"Poverty and Christian heroism are here," she wrote to Mother Sophie, and also bitter cold, hard work, lack of money and food, and active hostility toward the nuns—everything to try the soul of the most zealous missionary. But Philippine thrived on it. Always in the back of her mind was her determination to live with the Native Americans.

Within eight years after their landing in St. Charles, Philippine had established six more schools and orphanages, from St. Louis to New Orleans. The years passed, sixteen of them, and she continued her work with no let up of passion and persistence. Still, her life seemed to her to be littered with failures and disappointments. Schools she had opened up for the poor were closed and others were built that attracted the children of the well-to-do. She was often scorned and given little respect by her own sisters and the clergy in charge, and this must have hurt her feisty, independent spirit. And we can only imagine the struggle of this intense, certain-she-was-right woman to obey orders she did not feel were right.

By the age of seventy, weariness, poor health and old age had blurred her vision and diminished her confidence. When Mother Sophie wanted her to become the superior of a new foundation in Louisiana, Philippine wrote that she would rather not because,

> Here, more than in France, the old and ugly are held in low repute. I grow more unsightly every day. Gray hair, no teeth, horribly roughened hands, all make me in no way suitable to cut a figure in that fastidious section of the country…I carry in my heart a great fear of spoiling things wherever I shall be, and this because of words…I heard in the depths of my soul: "You are destined to please Me, not so much by success as by bearing failure"…and so I dread undertaking anything lest I should hinder its success.

Then, at the age of seventy-one, God gave her the gift she had already dismissed as never happening—her childhood wish. A Jesuit priest was opening a mission for the Native Americans at Sugar Creek, Kansas, and invited Philippine and four other sisters to come along and start a school. Philippine was elated, but some in charge wondered if she should go. She was not in good health, so what good could she be to the mission?

The Jesuit said firmly, "But she must come…even if she can use only one leg, she will come…if we have to carry her all the way on our shoulders, she is coming with us! She may not be able to do much work, but she will assure success to the mission by praying for us. Her very presence will draw down all manner of heavenly favors."

And so they set off, traveling up the Mississippi to Sugar Creek. They were met along the way by five hundred Natives in full tribal dress and brought to the village of seven hundred more, among them—tribes of Potawatomi, Kickapoo, Wabash and Osage.

Philippine was contented as she could be, even though she could do little more than visit the sick and teach the young girls sewing and knitting. Her main job, as the Jesuit foretold, was to pray, and that she did relentlessly, often for long stretches on her knees. The Native Americans called her

Woman-Who-Prays-Always. The legend is that as Philippine knelt and prayed, the children sneaked behind her and sprinkled bits of paper onto her habit. When they came back hours later, the paper was still there, unmoved.

Philippine enjoyed her life there but yearned for more. She wrote Mother Sophie,

> There are many saints buried in the little Indian cemetery.... I always go there...and beg of God the favor of being buried beside them. I feel, however, the same longing for the Rocky Mountain missions....They say in the Rockies people live to be a hundred years old....As I am only seventy-three...I think I shall have at least ten more years to work....Reverend Mother, will you not authorize me to go farther west...?

Mother Sophie would not. Then, another disappointment—Philippine was called back to St. Charles. Here she spent the last ten years of her life. We don't know how she filled them—in simple things, no doubt, the small offerings of daily routine, and, always, praying. She said, near the end of her life, "We cultivate a very small field for Christ, but we love it, knowing that God does not require great achievements but a heart that holds back nothing for self.... The truest crosses are those we do not choose ourselves...."

How well she knew! Thwarted and disappointed, Philippine nonetheless carried on, certain that God's hand was guiding the ups and downs. She is an example for all of us. Like the artist Vincent Van Gogh, who sold only one painting in his lifetime, like the poets Emily Dickinson and Gerard Manley Hopkins, who never saw their work published in their lifetime, Philippine's gifts went unnoticed while she lived. But in God's good time, when the world was ripe and ready, her legacy burst into bloom for all to appreciate.

Philippine died at the age of eighty-three on the feast of All Saints, a very good day to be welcomed home.

ANNE-THERESE GUERIN

When Anne-Therese was a little girl in Brittany in 1805, she often sat on the rocky ledges near her home and watched the ocean waves surge and recede on the shore below. She thought about the many things she did not know and could not see, like England and the New World, beyond the horizon of the English Channel. She wondered about the people who lived in these lands. Did they know God, did they speak with him as she did, and if so, what language did they speak?

Anne-Therese knew all about God because her mother had taught her about him and read her the Gospels. When she made her First Communion at the age of ten, she told the priest that she was going to spend the rest of her life serving God, and as she grew older, that desire grew stronger. But her plans had to be put aside when her father, an officer in the French navy on his way home on leave, was murdered by a bandit.

Life changed, and she grew up quickly. The next several years were spent taking care of her mother and younger sister, tending to business affairs, the gardens and the house. Her yearning to enter the convent would have to wait. She knew her mother was reluctant to let her go because she was such a dependable solace. But one evening she said to Anne-Therese, "My daughter, you may leave now; you have your mother's consent and blessing. I can no longer refuse God the sacrifice that he asks of me."

And so, a few months before her twenty-fifth birthday, Anne-Therese entered the convent of the Sisters of Providence of Ruille-sur-Loir, a community who worked as teachers and cared for the poor. Anne-Therese took the name of Sister Saint Theodore.

While she was in the novitiate, she became very ill—some say it was smallpox—and she feared her life of serving God would be a short one. Fortunately, a remedy was found, but it was a mixed blessing. The medicine that saved her life also damaged her digestive system so badly she could never again eat solid food. For the rest of her life, she existed on soft, bland foods and liquids. (Imagine not being able to bite into an apple or a wedge of pizza *ever*.)

A year after she professed her final vows—she was now Mother Theodore—she served as superior of the convent at Rennes, a city filled with many poor and unhappy victims of the aftermath of the French Revolution. Mother Theodore turned things around slowly. Little by little the children were brought back to church and learned their faith. The children changed and grew in hope, and smiles replaced scowls. The changes affected their families, and then the entire parish. Mother Theodore was praised for having worked a quiet miracle.

After Rennes, she went on to Soulaines, as superior of the convent there, and here she discovered a gift she didn't know she had. Besides her teaching, she went on regular visits to the sick poor with a local doctor. Her presence gave them spiritual comfort, but as she listened and observed, she was learning as well. Soon her knowledge of medicine and treatments became as important to her as her teaching.

Mother Theodore's next assignment was a big one. The bishop of Vincennes, Indiana, in the New World, had asked the Sisters of Providence to come and teach and care for the poor in his diocese. Indiana had few priests and many French, Irish and German immigrants in their congregations. He needed help, as soon as possible.

Mother Theodore was asked to lead this mission. At first she was not sure she was up to such a responsibility. She said she had to think about it. She made a list of reasons pro and con but still wrestled with her decision. Then she remembered a sentence from the congregation's Rule: "The Sisters will be disposed to go to any part of the world." Any part. That would include Vincennes, Indiana. She said yes.

So in July of 1840, Mother Theodore and five other nuns left the port of Le Havre to sail for the New World. She wrote in her journal: "The moment of separation...had come at last. We had to leave all. After having made the most painful sacrifices, which had cost our hearts so much, we had to break the last ties by tearing ourselves away from our dear 'Providence' of Ruille, that home so tenderly loved...."

After a voyage that lasted the summer, they arrived in New York City in September. But their journey was not over. They continued by stagecoach, steamboat and canal boat and in October reached their destination of Saint-Mary-of-the-Woods in Indiana.

> We continued to advance into the thick woods, till
> suddenly Father Buteux stopped the carriage and said,
> "Come down, Sisters, we have arrived." What was our
> astonishment to find ourselves still in the midst of the

forest, no village, not even a house in sight. Our guide led us down into a ravine, whence we beheld…a frame house with a stable and some sheds. "There," he said, "is the house…where you will lodge…."

In late November, the diocese purchased the house and the land around it, which would become the foundation for the Sisters of Providence of Saint-Mary-of-the-Woods. Eight months later, the sisters opened their first academy for girls, and within a year, two more schools were built in Jasper, Indiana, and St. Francisville, Illinois.

For the next fourteen years, Mother Theodore's mission of teaching and healing grew and expanded across Indiana— twelve schools, two orphanages, several pharmacies where the sick and poor could obtain free medicines, and their congregation had grown from the original six to sixty-seven professed sisters.

Mother Theodore died at the age of fifty-eight in 1856 and is buried in the Church of the Immaculate Conception at Saint-Mary-of-the-Woods. Pope John Paul II has given her the title of Venerable, in recognition of "a virtuous life lived to a heroic degree."

Compared to Philippine Duchesne's life, Mother Theodore's seems such a quietly heroic adventure—steadfast, without great stress, strain or melodrama. She came to the New World because she believed this is what God wanted of her, and she did her work without apparent disappointment or failure. But only God knows the sacrifices she made to achieve such calm and resolve, and it's between them. (But one can wonder, for instance, how she managed the pitching and rolling of that ocean voyage, having a queasy stomach to begin with!)

Still, these two pioneers have as many similarities as differences. Both were born in France, and although Philippine was thirty years old when Anne-Therese was born, they lived during the same time, became nuns, worked to heal the emotional and physical ravages left by the French Revolution, became missionaries to the New World, built schools and orphanages and planted their orders firmly in the soil where they bloom today, and died here within four years of each other.

Did these two women ever cross paths while in the New World? If so, surely they would have been good friends!

DAMIEN OF MOLOKAI

When the sixth child of Catherine and François de Veuster was born on a wintry January night in 1840, there was the usual joy and excitement that a new baby had joined their family. The villagers of Tremeloo, their farming community in northern Belgium, came by with casseroles, fresh sweet buns and knitted booties to admire the newborn and toast him with beer and wine. Another farmer for Tremeloo who would be toasting *his* son some day! For, of course, he would stay. The citizens of Tremeloo rarely left, content with their lives, which were as constant as the seasons. Why would anyone want to leave Tremeloo?

Joseph de Veuster felt the same way during his childhood filled with the pleasant routines of work and school and play with his brothers and sisters. He loved everything physical—climbing trees, rough-and-tumble pranks, ice-skating on the river Laak, in everything always competitive. He had to win!

School ended for him at the age of thirteen for he had to help his father on the farm. He sought out the chore of tending the sheep, for here he could satisfy the other quiet side of him and his growing need for solitude.

As the sheep grazed, he would stretch out on the riverbank and stare into the sky, curious about the world beyond it and the God who lived there. Why was he, Joseph, here? What was he supposed to do with his life? Would he be content as a farmer?

An answer came with his father's decision that Joseph, who had a quick, organized mind, good with figures, should further his education.

He was sent to school in Braine-le-Compt, in southern Belgium, for commercial studies. Now this was akin to studying in a foreign country, for there were many differences between northern and southern Belgium. Even the language was different. At home he spoke Flemish; at school he had to learn French. There was a snobbish scorn of the northerners, and Joseph had to endure cruel teasing about his being a thick hick and a clodhopper from the boonies—but not for long. Joseph had grown into a handsome young man with curly dark hair, a healthy physique and a quick temper. He fought back with an intensity that brought an immediate ceasefire and instant respect!

After a while he began to enjoy his life at school and his visits with his brother, Auguste, who was in the novitiate of the Congregation of the Sacred Hearts of Jesus and Mary in Paris. Joseph envied his brother who glowed with enthusiasm for his new life. If only he could feel that way about being a businessman!

Gradually, he began to realize that he wanted to join Auguste. But how could he tell his parents? They would be hurt and upset; they were counting on him to come home. He gathered his courage and wrote them a careful, practical letter, commenting first on his sister's becoming a nun: "What happiness is hers! She has made sure of the most difficult thing, which we have to perform in this life....I hope my turn will come to choose the path I ought to tread. Would it not be possible for me to follow my brother...?"

He was right. They *were* hurt and upset. But he persisted. He wrote to them again a few months later at Christmas, "This great feast has brought me to quit the world and embrace the religious state....Therefore, my dear parents, I implore you again for your consent...."

This time, he got it. A week later, on his nineteenth birthday, Joseph settled in with his brother at the novitiate in Louvain, ready to begin a life of service to God, wherever it might be. Because he had no education in classical languages, he worked as a lay brother. He didn't care. Whatever job was given to him, he did it with zest. With his physical strength and quiet perseverance, he was in demand for the order's building projects. His hammer, it was said, was as dear to him as his breviary.

He seemed to know no fear. Once when ground needed to be cleared for a new building, a tall chimney had to be torn down. The chimney was a dangerous, unstable object, which swayed at the slightest touch. No sensible workman would go near it. Joseph said simply that they should stand back, and he climbed the quivering chimney and carefully removed the bricks, one at a time, all the way down.

Auguste began tutoring him in Latin, which would help him to become a priest, and it was tough going. Joseph was a good, steadfast scholar, but not a brilliant one. Yet, he plodded on until the goal of ordination was within his grasp. Then came word that the bishop of Hawaii had made a plea to the Superior General of their order for missionaries to work in Oceania, the former name of the islands of the central and south Pacific. There was a great need for workers to bring God's word to the natives of these tropical lands, and Joseph—

now known by his religious name, Damien—knew in his bones that this was why he was here, that this faraway paradise was where he was meant to be. Auguste felt the same way and was immediately selected. Damien was not, and he was deeply disappointed. But he put aside his sadness to help his brother prepare for the trip.

But God's plan for the brothers turned theirs upside down. Damien went and Auguste didn't. A typhus epidemic swept through Louvain, and Auguste was one of its victims. Although he recovered, he was not well enough to make the long ocean voyage. Damien begged the Superior General to let him go instead. The Superior General sat silently, observing the trembling would-be missionary, and then said sternly, "It is rather foolish for you to want to go before you are a priest, but you have your wish. You are to go!" Damien wept for joy.

He was twenty-three years old when he and his fellow missionaries left the port of Bremerhaven, Germany, in October 1963 for a voyage that would last five months on a three-masted merchant ship. He enjoyed the disciplined routine of ship life and the exhilaration of climbing up the rigging with the sailors, resting above the sails, Master of the Seas! But these same seas could and did turn wildly terrifying in January as they rounded Cape Horn.

Mountains of churning waves crashed and drenched the boat from both sides, as the missionaries and nuns down below prayed with all their hearts for their survival. On the tenth day, as if by some heavenly signal, serenity returned, and the winds turned to warm, obedient breezes and remained so for the rest of the trip. When they first sighted the mountains of Hawaii on the horizon, a great cheer went up with cries of "Hurrah! We made it!" and the anticipation for what awaited them was exhilarating.

They were not disappointed! Startling sights, sounds and smells greeted them. Golden-skinned natives, who welcomed them with flowers, fruit and songs. Lush trees, greenery and plants they did not know. The variety of faces on the crowded streets. The writer John Farrow, described this "kaleidoscope of wonders": "bare-footed native urchins...the faces of Chinese immigrants, the kimonos of Japanese women, sun-blackened fishermen...red-faced English blue jackets and lantern-jawed Yankee merchants...." How, Damien wondered, would he fit in here?

Two months later, after he was ordained, he found out. He was twenty-three, filled with zeal and ready for anything. He was assigned to parishes on several of the Hawaiian Islands, where he learned the language and the customs of the people who lived there. "I liked them immensely," he wrote his brother, "you could not wish for better people, so gentle, pleasant-mannered, exceedingly tender-hearted are they...they are ready to deprive themselves even of necessaries in order to supply your every want." Their good will and Damien's honest love for them made many converts.

By the time he was twenty-five, Damien had served on all the islands except one, the dreaded, isolated settlement of Molokai, otherwise known as "the island of lepers." At that time, the disease of leprosy—even the name was whispered with a shiver—was spreading through Hawaii as a powerful, unstoppable epidemic. It was an ancient disease of mysterious origin, which made it even more fearful. Doctors knew only two things for certain: it was contagious and it was incurable. So the government took drastic measures: Anyone suspected of having the disease was rounded up by the police, often torn from his or her family and put on the boat to Molokai.

Here no doctors, homes or care awaited them. They were simply dumped into the surf and left to wade ashore and fend for themselves. Many were often too sick to make a home or find food and they just died. Their bodies were thrown into shallow graves or left for wild dogs or pigs to finish off.

Leprosy was not a disease one could hide. It could turn healthy people into repulsive creatures by bloating and disfiguring their bodies and faces. Often toes, fingers, ears, limbs rotted away and fell off. Eye sockets became "craters of pus," open sores oozed and gave off a foul odor. They were the "unclean" and unwanted, and the sooner they were out of sight and mind, the better.

The situation weighed heavily on the bishop of Hawaii's heart. He knew they needed care, and he knew that any priest he sent to them would not come back. He decided, in a homily, to share his problem and ask for a volunteer priest. As soon as he stopped speaking, four priests stood up, and Damien was one of them.

Damien argued that despite his youth, he should be the one sent to the island. He was experienced in working with the natives and wanted to spend his life with them. The bishop, with tears in his eyes, said, "I would not have imposed this on anyone, but I gladly accept your offer."

They left that evening. The bishop, Damien and fifty lepers headed for the dreaded island aboard a steamer. The next morning Damien saw the rocky coastline of Molokai, forbidding as a prison. A crowd of lepers was waiting to greet him on shore. What Damien found made him angry, as well as sad. He could not believe that human beings could be dumped here like garbage, with no thought as to how they would survive. That first night he slept beneath a pandanus tree that grew next to the graveyard. He lit his pipe and leaned against the tree trunk, thinking of the work he had to do when dawn came.

That morning he began the first steps in making Molokai a real community, one with hope, compassion, pride and even song and laughter. These were *his* people, and he, *Kamiano*, as they called him, was their father now. He also became their doctor, judge, lawyer, counselor, disciplinarian, builder and architect. Whatever they needed, Kamiano supplied.

He also was a huge bother to the government, for he was always pestering them for necessary things: food, money, lumber, pipes, building and medical supplies. With stubborn persistence, he would not be ignored, until finally, to get rid of him, the government granted him everything he asked for. Soon the residents of Molokai had their own whitewashed cottages, each with its own garden patch for vegetables and flowers. He laid pipe from a spring in the woods so the lepers could have fresh water from taps built near their homes. And he showed no fear or repulsion in showing them comfort, in shaking their hands, dressing their wounds. Sometimes he would have to leave a cottage to breathe in fresh air. His pipe, he said, was his salvation because it cleansed the putrid smell from his clothes.

In the evening, when he ate his meal outside his own one-room dwelling, the islanders would come and encircle him. They would tell stories, jokes and even sing. He in turn would tell them tales of a faraway world in Belgium and about life on a ship in a storm. These gatherings, just before dusk, became such a custom they even had a name, the "Time of peace between night and day."

Damien had been pastor of his people for eleven years when he discovered the first telltale spots on his skin. In his homilies, he always addressed his congregation as "we lepers." Now he was truly one of them. He worked furiously while he was able, knowing his time was limited. He built two schools, an orphanage and a new chapel. New helpers came, inspired by stories of Damien's work. (Word of his work had been spread by visitors and his own letters that had found their way into newspapers around the world.) Famous writers and artists came to visit him and have left us with portraits of this complex man, who died at the age of forty-nine, after serving Molokai for sixteen years.

Damien was many things to many people: a loving, obedient

son, a solitary contemplative and a man of action who was impatient to get things done, quick to anger, quick to remorse, obstinate, cranky, blunt and headstrong, a bother, an annoyance. Some thought of him as a hero, others thought he was crazy. When Pope John Paul II beatified Damien in 1995, he reminded us that "holiness is not perfection according to human criteria; it is not reserved for a small amount of exceptional persons. It is for everyone...."

Robert Louis Stevenson wrote, that if Damien were indeed an imperfect man, "with all the grime and paltriness of mankind, he was still a saint and hero all the more for that."

KATHARINE DREXEL

Have you ever daydreamed about what it would be like to have everything you want? To never have to work and wait and save for a bike or college or sneakers with reflector lights? To wake up one morning and decide to sail to France that day or ride your own train to the Rockies? To have enough money so you never have to think about money?

We know some people are born into such a life. It would be easy to envy them because their lives seem so easy. But when we remember our Lord's warning that it is easier for a camel to pass through the eye of a needle than for a rich man to get into heaven, we realize that they may have to struggle even harder than we do to become saints. And becoming saints is why all of us, rich or poor, are here.

This is the story of Katharine Drexel, who always knew the

important thing in life wasn't having money, it was pleasing God. She was born in 1858 to Francis Drexel, a wealthy Philadelphia banker, and his wife, Hannah, a Quaker, who died when Katharine was five weeks old. She had an older sister, Elizabeth, and, after her father remarried two years later, a younger one, Louise.

The sisters were inseparable; they truly loved and delighted in each other. Their stepmother, Emma Bouvier, was as devoted to Elizabeth and Katharine as she was to Louise, and they returned her love.

Yes, you could say this was a family that was blessed with all the good things of life. They had a winter mansion in Philadelphia and a summer estate in nearby Torresdale, with their own private chapel and a statue of Saint Michael carved in stone at the entrance. They had private tutors, each for a different subject, and traveled to Europe regularly to visit art museums and cathedrals and the pope. The girls were very much part of the social whirl and wore the most stylish gowns and diamonds in their ears at the coming-out parties.

You would expect them to have been spoiled, selfish children. Yet, they were as good and kind as they were privileged. Their parents believed they were stewards of God's gifts, which were to be shared wisely. Three afternoons a week they opened their home to the poor and needy. They gave money, clothing and medicine lovingly and graciously so that those in need would not feel like beggars.

Francis Drexel went to Mass early each morning and often played the organ as little Kate sat quietly, soaking it all up. And every evening there were family prayers and the rosary, and parental reminders that although they lived in a garden of earthly delights now, these pleasures did not last. They might enjoy them as a traveler enjoys the glorious sights along a journey, but they were not to forget the destination of their journey—heaven.

Katharine took these things to heart. As a teenager, she worried (perhaps too much) about displeasing God. She kept a journal of resolutions to root out her weaknesses:

> *Pride and Vanity*
> April—The same. Did not try to overcome.
> May—Bad, not trying to overcome.
> June—I never tried.
> July, August, September—Bad!

And on December 31, 1881, her new year's resolutions included:

> No cake for 1882
> No preserves until June 1882
> No grapes, no honey until July 1st.

Like Thérèse, the "little flower," she would make no lukewarm sacrifices!

When Katharine was twenty-five, the family's sunny existence changed. First, her beloved stepmother died. Then, two years later, her father died, leaving the sisters with an inheritance of fourteen million dollars to be divided among them. Despite their sadness, they rejoiced at this opportunity to carry on their parents' generosity.

Each of the sisters used the money for a personal charity. Elizabeth bought land at Eddington, Pennsylvania, and built the St. Francis de Sales Industrial School for young black men, in honor of Francis Drexel. Louise gave a gift of land to the Josephite Fathers in Baltimore, Maryland, on which they built Epiphany College, and also, near Richmond, Virginia, built St. Emma's Industrial and Agricultural Institute, in honor of her stepmother.

Katharine's special enthusiasm was for the welfare of the Native Americans. As a child she believed that Columbus discovered America specifically to save the natives' souls, and she, being a patriotic American, wanted to do her part. She began immediately by giving money for schools and missions to be built for the native children of the Dakotas.

The sisters decided to travel to Europe to learn about setting up schools and new educational training methods. And, once they built the schools, they needed to find priests who would be willing to come and teach in them. At monastery after monastery, they were turned down. Disappointed, they went on to the climax of their trip, an audience with Pope Leo XIII in Rome.

Kneeling at the pope's feet, Katharine asked for his help in finding missionaries for the natives, certain that he would not refuse her help. To her surprise he said, "Why not, my child, yourself become a missionary?"

This hit a nerve in her soul because, unknown to anyone, she had been struggling with the question of how she would spend her life. She knew it would be in the service of God, but was it to be in a convent as a contemplative nun (which was the kind of religious life she yearned for), or in the wealthy social world in which she was already comfortable, where she could marry and have a family and continue her charitable work?

Her conflict was still unresolved when they returned from Europe. She put it aside as the sisters made plans to visit some of the missions out west. The trip was quite an adventure. They went by train from Philadelphia to Omaha, then by carriage (which was really a wagon) and horseback across the prairies to South Dakota, where they saw for themselves the hard life and conditions of the Sioux people. Here they met the famous Sioux chief, Red Cloud, who was impressed by these caring white women.

When Katharine returned to Philadelphia, she immediately began drawing up plans for more boarding schools for these children who had become so dear to her. Within five years, she had founded schools from the Northwest Territories to the Mexican border. Not just one tribe but many—Sioux, Nez

Perce, Chippewas, Crows, Blackfeet, Cherokee, Pueblo, Navajo—shared in the bounty of Katharine's stewardship.

And all the while, Katharine still hadn't made up her mind what to do with her life. Finally, after much soul-searching (she even wrote down on paper, in two columns, her reasons for and against becoming a nun), she came to her decision. She wrote in her journal:

> The question then of my state in life resolves itself…into this one. What can I do for God's greater glory and service? I assume He wishes me to be where I can first save my own soul, secondly, to do as much good as He intends with the means Dear Papa has left me. If Our Lord wishes me to go to a convent, I should be an idiot did I not obey the call.… If amongst the temptations of the world, it is His will that I should steer my course, to heaven, fiat.…To tell the truth, it appears to me that God calls me to the religious life.…

The next question was: which order? She wanted to find a missionary order that worked with Native Americans. And the words of the pope came back to her. Why not start her own order for this specific purpose? She was convinced this was to be her particular work.

But first she would be trained in the religious life at the novitiate at the Sisters of Mercy convent in Pittsburgh. After three years there, she made plans to build the motherhouse of her new order, the Sisters of the Blessed Sacrament for Indians and Colored People (which is what the Native American and black community was called at that time). While she and the first thirteen novices waited for the motherhouse to be built outside Philadelphia, they lived at the Drexel summer home, which was now empty. (Katharine's two sisters had married.) How bittersweet the memories must have been for Katharine, remembering the happy days with her family.

Finally the day arrived, February 12, 1891, when Katharine became Mother Katharine Drexel. To her vows of poverty, chastity and obedience, she added, "to be the mother and servant of the Indian and Negro races according to the rule of the Sisters of the Blessed Sacrament."

After three years of training, she sent the first group of her nuns out to teach in Santa Fe, New Mexico. This began forty years of missionary work under her leadership—traveling, planning, promoting, staffing (she finally did find an order of priests, the Franciscan Fathers of the Cincinnati Province), financing and directing the administration of her order. In the year of her death, 1955, her order numbered 502 sisters, who were conducting sixty-one schools for African and Native Americans in thirteen states.

It wasn't a smooth trip. She learned quickly that not everyone was as eager to educate children of color as she was. As early as July 16, 1891, a day of public celebration when the nuns first put on the new habits of their order, there were threats and rumors of dynamite being found and that "all Catholics on the platform would be blown to hell."

Fortunately, nothing happened that day, but a continuous threat hung over her and her sisters whenever a new opportunity (or challenge) presented itself. She accepted the danger from those crippled by fear and prejudice, and it didn't stop her. She prayed for the courage to do what was right, and then she did it.

In Nashville, Mother Katharine bought a building that she wanted to use for an Industrial Academy for Colored Girls. When news of this got around, the neighbors were indignant. The former owner offered to give her back the purchase price if she would just go away. Mother Katharine replied by letter in her dignified, polite way:

> I hasten to express to you my regret that you and your neighbors should feel as you do concerning the purchase of property.... The Sisters of the Blessed Sacrament...are religious, of the same race as yourself. We will always

endeavor in every way to be neighborly to any white
neighbors in the vicinity; we have every reason to hope we
may receive from our white neighbors the cordial courtesy
for which the Southern people are so justly noted....

It didn't help. The only response was a letter from a group of
Nashville women concerned that the opening of such a school
would depreciate their property. Mother Katharine went ahead
with her plans, and on September 5, 1905, the school was
opened with thirty-eight students enrolled. She recorded her
thoughts:

Resolve: with no half-hearted, timorous dread of the
opinions of Church and men to manifest my mission. To
speak only and when it pleases God, but to lose no
opportunity of speaking before priests and bearded men....
You have no time to occupy your thoughts with that
complacency or consideration of what others will think.
Your business is simply, "What will my Father in Heaven
think?"

In 1915, when the archbishop of New Orleans asked Mother
Katharine to bring her sisters to start a college there, she met
this challenge with pleasure. Because of segregation, there was
no opportunity for black high school graduates to continue
their education. She found a spacious, abandoned college
building in the center of a city square, shaded by huge old oak
trees, which would be perfect.

Again, she was met by anger and resentment from neighbors.
One of her deepest beliefs was that the educated man or
woman was anyone's equal, regardless of skin color. She had to
prove this belief in a segregated society, which she could not
change, working within its limitations as best she could.

By September 15, 1915, the words "Xavier University" were
cut into stone above the entrance. There were three hundred
full-time students and one hundred afternoon and evening

classes in sewing and typewriting. By 1924, Xavier University was established as a College of Liberal Arts and Sciences; in 1927 a College of Pharmacy was added. Today, graduates of Xavier have made their mark all over the world as musicians, writers, artists, scientists and educators. And it is truly integrated, with people of all races as part of the student body and faculty.

In 1935, at the age of seventy-seven, Mother Katharine retired as founder of the Sisters of the Blessed Sacrament and began her new vocation, one she had yearned for many years ago. For the next twenty years, she lived a life centered in prayer. From her room on the second floor of the motherhouse, she took on the problems and needs of all those in the small world surrounding her, then reached out to include worlds across oceans. She prayed for her sisters, for world leaders, for the young soldiers fighting World War II on both sides; she prayed for the sick, for the abandoned, for those who needed prayers *right now*. She even prayed for Hitler.

And most of all, she prayed for her black and Native American children. One evening, near the end of her life, she called to the sister who was taking care of her.

"Come quickly, Sister," she said. "Did you see them?"

"See what?" asked the puzzled sister.

"The children! Oh, all the children were there, going past, so many of them. And the pope was there too. Look, there they are!" she exclaimed, her eyes on the ceiling.

Perhaps they were the thousands of children who learned about God and their special gifts because of her. No doubt they lined the road and cheered when she arrived in heaven on March 3, 1955, at the age of ninety-seven!

Mother Katharine Drexel was beatified on November 20, 1988, and was canonized on October 1, 2000, by Pope John Paul II.

JOSEPHINE BAKHITA

All saints' stories are adventure stories, even if the saints never leave their homes, convents, prisons or huts in the wood. For the adventures that lead to their holiness take place in their minds and souls. They use the circumstances of their lives right where they are.

There are also those saints who have real, live adventures traveling the unexpected path God has laid out for them, and one of these saints was Bakhita.

Bakhita was the daughter of a well-to-do family in the village of Algoznei in Eastern Sudan in Africa. Her uncle was the tribal chief, her father owned land and cattle. She lived a happy, carefree life with her parents, brothers and sisters. Although they were not Christians, they belonged to an African religion, which believed in a mysterious and powerful presence that was found in all creation. Bakhita yearned to know this power, this mystery, who had made earth and sky.

"Seeing the sun, the moon and the stars, I said to myself, 'Who could be the master of these beautiful things?' I felt a great desire to see him…and to pay him homage."

This happy, comfortable life came to an abrupt end when slave-traders captured her while she was playing in a field. She was only nine years old. Bakhita, which means "the lucky one" (we don't know her real name; this is the name that was given to her by her captors) was now the property of the slave-traders and was sold at slave markets many times over in different cities. She endured incredible hardships. Long marches that went on for weeks, beatings, scraps for food and being chained to the wall in dark cells with dirt floors.

Bakhita recalled how she survived those years as a slave, "I would lie on the ground in a kind of stupor," imagining and remembering life with loved ones—laughing and playing with friends and she would live in this remembered world to ease her sadness.

Once, when Bakhita's owner forgot to lock her door, she and another girl escaped. They ran and ran, through fields and forests, streams and desert, until they were exhausted. "We knew our hope…rested upon the speed of our young legs… we could hear the roaring of wild beasts echoing in the darkness…when animals approached, the best we could do was run for a tree and climb it."

Unfortunately, they were caught, and Bakhita was sold to an Arab chief, whose son beat her so severely she could not work for a month. The chief sold her to a Turkish general who bought her as a personal maid for his mother and wife. For three years Bakhita attended to their every desire, doing her best to please, but rarely succeeding. If she accidentally pinched them or pulled their hair, she would be whipped, and "when a wound from the whip began to heal, other blows would pour down on me."

When she was fourteen, she was sold yet again, this time to the Italian consul in Sudan. Her new master was kind and she was not beaten or punished. For the first time since she was kidnapped, she knew some peace. She felt she was truly "the lucky one." After two years, the consul was recalled to Italy. Bakhita was mysteriously drawn to this country of her master—if all the people there were kind like him, what a marvelous place it must be! She begged to go with him. At first he said no, for it was a long journey, but she persisted, and he finally gave in. In the back of his mind, the consul had the thought that once in Italy, he would free her.

They traveled by camel to a port on the Red Sea and there boarded the ship to Italy. Can you imagine the excitement and wonder of the young woman on her first sea voyage? The smell and sound of the ocean, the cries and patterns of flying birds, the sight of stars and moon sparkling on the black waves, left her in awe as always of the Power that created them.

Among the passengers Bakhita met was a friend of the consul, Mr. Michieli. When they arrived in Genoa, Mrs. Michieli was waiting for her husband, and she too met and was charmed by Bakhita. "Why didn't you bring *me* an African girl to be our new nanny?" she complained jokingly, but half meaning it. The Michieli's baby was expected soon, and the consul felt they needed Bakhita more than he did, so he gave Bakhita to her. Bakhita was sad to leave her benefactor, but she didn't refuse or question his decision. After all, she was just a slave and had no rights.

A little girl, Mimmina, was born to the Michielis and Bakhita became her nursemaid and constant companion. After three years, the Michielis and Bakhita returned to Africa, for Mr. Michieli owned a large hotel there. Nine months later, Mrs. Michieli, Mimmina and Bakhita returned to Italy to sell their property and settle affairs so they could live permanently in Africa. While this was happening, Mimmina, now five, and

Bakhita, twenty-one, were sent to a boarding school in Venice run by the Canossian Sisters of Charity.

This opened a brand new world for Bakhita, for here she discovered the Creator she had longed to know and the faith into which she would be baptized. It fulfilled all her wonderings and yearnings. "The dear saintly sisters...helped me know God," she said, "whom I had experienced in my heart since childhood, without knowing who He was..."

Her new "Master" gave her the grace to make a difficult decision. For most of her life, she had been a slave, her only purpose in life to serve others at their will and whim. They had determined what she did, wore, ate, when she woke and when she slept. Now God had given her the courage to change all that.

When Mrs. Michieli told Bakhita that it was time to go back to Africa, Bakhita refused. She wanted to stay with the sisters. Mrs. Michieli and Mimmina were stunned. They pleaded and cried and threatened, but Bakhita would not budge. "It was painful," she said, "I felt so unhappy...to see her upset and angry because I really loved her. I am sure the Lord gave me a special strength at that moment..."

Mrs. Michieli was determined to have her way. She called on the King's procurator for help and was told that slavery was illegal in Italy and Bakhita could do as she liked. Mrs. Michieli was so angry she snatched Mimmina from Bakhita's arms as they were saying goodbye and stomped off. Bakhita knew she had lost another family, but this time it was by her choice.

Two months later she was baptized in the Canossian chapel and given the name Josephine. She wanted to stay with the sisters and become one of them, for she "could hear, more and more clearly, the gentle voice of the Lord, urging me to consecrate my life to Him," but she hesitated. Would the sisters welcome a black woman, a slave? What did she have to offer?

She went to the Mother General, confiding her desire and doubts. "I see only Italian sisters in the convent," she said. "Nonsense," the Mother General reassured her. "Of course you can join us. Why ever not?!"

And so, in 1893, Josephine entered the novitiate of the Canossian sisters in Venice, and made her vows in 1896 in Verona. On the day of her profession, she prayed, "Dear Lord, could I but fly to Africa and proclaim aloud to all my people your goodness to me. How many souls would hear my voice and turn to you: my dear Mamma and Papa, my brothers, my sisters…all the poor people of Africa. Grant…that they may know and love you!"

For the next fifty years Josephine served wherever she was needed in whatever work was given, all done in the quiet confidence of "I try to do my best; He does all the rest." By her standards, she was very ordinary. She had no great gifts of prophecy, no visions and she never indulged in harsh forms of penance. She simply served her Master, as she called God, by doing the work of the day.

Josephine lived with the nuns of Venice for six years and then was transferred to Schio, in northern Italy, where she was the cook at a boarding school for girls. During World War I, the school became a military hospital. While most of the sisters and students left for another home, Josephine and a few other nuns stayed behind to help with the wounded soldiers. Like a mother, she was kind and compassionate when they needed it, but she put them in their place and told them to mind their manners when they were rowdy.

After the war, when the school returned to normal, Josephine was assigned the job of portress, or doorkeeper. She opened the door every morning when the youngest children came with their mothers for kindergarten. She became good friends with the mothers who confided their problems to her sympathetic ear and asked for her advice.

Then the sisters asked Josephine to make a lecture tour to tell the story of her life. It would be her chance to be a missionary of sorts, they said. Josephine, who loved her quiet, anonymous life, dreaded speaking in public for all to view. But she had promised her Master to do whatever he asked, so she prayed he would give her all the skill she needed.

So off she went, visiting all the Canossian convents in Italy, speaking to spellbound audiences who might have come out of curiosity to see the black nun, "Mother Moretta," but who left remembering not her color but her message: "Be grateful to God and Our Lady.... Love the Lord, pray for the unhappy souls who do not yet know Him. What a great grace it is to know God!"

By 1938, Josephine was seventy-two years old and in frail health. Soon another war would be ravaging Europe, but this time the sisters stayed put and did not leave Schio. When air raid sirens would sound, Josephine calmly kept on with her work. "Let them fire away," she said, "it is the Master who is in command. Trust in God!" In the midst of the bombings, Josephine celebrated the fiftieth anniversary of becoming a nun, and the whole town came to the chapel to celebrate with her.

On February 8, 1947, *Bakhita, Sister Josephine, Mother Moretta*—slave, nanny, portress, teacher, lecturer, seamstress, cook—died of pneumonia.

This woman of gentle dignity, who used every bit of her talents to serve her Master, would finally meet him and Our Lady face to face and be welcomed as the royalty she was. Before she died, Josephine told her sisters, "I am sure I will not be rejected. Then I will turn to Saint Peter and say, 'You can close the door after me; I am here to stay!'"

SOLANUS CASEY

The childhood of Barney Casey could have been the script for a television series, a well-loved, heartwarming story right up there with *The Waltons* and *Little House on the Prairie*. There is something in us that yearns for these tales of good, hard-working folks, large happy families, cozy and safe, gathered around the hearth in their log cabins.

And the Casey family of Prescott, Wisconsin, was really that. The parents, Bernard and Ellen, were immigrants from Ireland who met and married in Salem, Massachusetts, and with their two young children, Ellen and James, decided to move west to Prescott and join Ellen's brother in farming. First they built a three-room log cabin on the banks of the Mississippi, and here five more children were born, including Barney.

The family needed more room so they moved on to a larger farm near the Trimbelle River. As Barney later described it, it was a place of valleys and prairies rolling down to the river, streams and ponds for fishing and swimming, and a pasture for cattle. (Eventually there were sixteen, with enough Casey boys to form their own baseball team—which they did!)

The family horse and wagon could not hold everyone all at once, so on Sundays, one parent would take half the children to Mass, and on the next Sunday, the other parent and children would go. Everyone's favorite time was evening after supper, after farm, house and school work were done, and they would gather to say the rosary, and the parents would tell tales of life in Ireland or read aloud from the novels of Sir Walter Scott or the poetry of Longfellow. And, after reading, Barney, ever ready, would play his violin with more joy than skill, until his brothers made him stop.

Balancing the sweet contentment were the hardships and sacrifices of pioneer life—the physical work from dawn to dusk, crop failures, locusts, snakes, wildcats, and worst of all, sickness. An epidemic of diphtheria took the lives of two Casey daughters and left Barney with damaged vocal cords, a weak, wispy voice and chronic sore throat.

The family prospered enough to move to a larger home, a 350-acre farm. Barney had to leave school for a while to work on the farm, and he didn't finish grammar school until he was seventeen. Then he left home to earn money and went up north to work as a log-roller (one who dislodged log jams and moved logs down the river to the sawmills). Then he went to Stillwater, Minnesota, where he made bricks by day and was a prison guard at the penitentiary by night. Here the compassion that came into full bloom when he was a friar showed itself in his treatment of the prisoners. He listened to them, and, young as he was, advised them as to how to better their lives. Two prisoners, members of the notorious Jesse James gang, took such a liking to him that one gave him a clothes trunk, which Barney took with him when he entered the monastery.

He continued trying different jobs, trying them on like new suits to see which one fit the best. He went next to Superior, Michigan, where he became a streetcar conductor. One day, he abruptly brought his trolley to a stop, for directly on the road ahead of him was the body of a young woman. She lay so quiet, her life bleeding away from many stab wounds inflicted by a drunken sailor. The scene shook Barney to the depths of his soul. In that instant, he saw how quickly life comes and goes. He realized he must do something with his life *now* and not wait for *someday*. For some time, he had had the thought that his purpose in life was to serve God, specifically as a priest, and that *someday* was now.

He asked the advice of a spiritual director, Father Vollmer, who suggested he go to the Seminary of St. Francis de Sales in Milwaukee. And that is what Barney did. He set off with a twenty-one-year-old's fervor and enthusiasm—which drizzled away once he got there. For one thing, his poor educational background made seminary life very difficult. For another, since the people of this area were of mostly German descent, the classes were taught in the German language. Latin was hard enough, but Latin taught in German was too much for him. For all his determination, Barney's grades began to slip and never recovered. His superiors decided he would never become a diocesan priest and suggested he try elsewhere.

Once again, Father Vollmer had a suggestion—why not try a Capuchin monastery? Barney didn't have high hopes, but he went to be polite. He came back thoroughly depressed and certain this was not for him. Again, most of the monks were German-speaking, and they wore long beards. Barney detested the beards. (Father Vollmer teased him, "Barney, you will love the Capuchin beard. It will keep you warm and protect your throat and chest!") Barney was not at all convinced. He prayed a novena to the Immaculate Conception to help him decide. On the last day, December 8, as he knelt in the chapel, he heard a voice in his soul, a voice he was sure was Mary's. It said, "Go to Detroit." It was a message he really did not want to hear. The Capuchin monastery was in Detroit.

But he had asked for a sign, and what could be more specific than these three words? He went home, told his family, packed his trunk and was ready to take on his new life. His parents urged him to wait until after Christmas—let them enjoy one last Christmas together—but he said God could not wait, and he left.

He arrived at the Capuchin monastery on Christmas Eve. It was a cold, bleak night outside, and not much warmer inside. He felt forlorn, cold, hungry, unwelcome, a stranger amongst the German monks. He lay down in his cell, covered himself with the thin blanket and let the tears flow. What was he doing here? Why did Our Lady lead him to this place? He already missed his family terribly. He thought he could not be any more depressed.

But within three weeks, all doubts had been put to rest. He was robed in the brown habit and sandals and given the name of Brother Francis Solanus. His next hurdle was his studies—again. No matter how hard he tried, his grades never rose to the height of *fair*. His superiors were befuddled as to what to do with him. They knew his deep spiritual and moral qualities more than balanced his poor grades, but they were afraid he might mislead the faithful if he did not understand theology correctly. Solanus knew how they felt and signed a statement of intention, saying "I have offered myself to God without reservation," and for that reason, he "left it to my superiors to decide what is best."

They decided to ordain him as a "simplex" priest, one who could say Mass but not preach or hear confessions. We don't know how Solanus felt about this, but we can imagine it must have hurt to be a priest—but not completely. But he showed nothing but pride and joy on the day of his ordination, which his proud family came to celebrate with him.

He was assigned to Sacred Heart parish in Yonkers, New York, where the pastor also wondered what to do with a priest who couldn't preach or hear confessions. He decided to give him charge of the sacristy and the altar boys. Barney threw himself into his work, and it *was* work, handling the lively and mischievous young boys. They were, as their mothers would say, a handful, so much so that Solanus made a novena to Our Lady of Perpetual Help for—*help*. He said his prayers had extraordinary results in calming them down!

Two years later, he was given an extra job as porter, or doorkeeper, and this is where his unique vocation began. Solanus opened the door not only to the friary but also to the hearts of those parched for God's love. All who entered here with a need—healing, money, a job, a broken family—were welcomed by Solanus and listened to as if each person were the only one in the world. He would bring the needy one into his office and serve him hot coffee and a thick slice of buttered bread, "as if we were royalty," one said. If anything went wrong in the neighborhood, people would say "Hurry, go get the holy priest!"

He calmed their fears, prayed with them, often healed them. And when he prayed with them, he would ask that they show their confidence by promising some prayer or sacrifice or good work in return, so they could be part of the healing process. He told them to thank God ahead of time for granting their requests, saying God could not resist their gratitude.

And when there were those he knew would not be healed here on earth, he gently prepared them for their entrance into heaven. Once when he visited a dying woman, she said, "Oh, you look just like Jesus...." Solanus replied, "Well, I'm taking his place....I've come to give you a crown."

It didn't matter to him whether the person was a Jew or Protestant or an atheist, for he believed the Holy Spirit healed everyone impartially. "Religion," he said, "is nothing less than the science of our happy relationship with God and our neighbors—then there can be but one religion, though there may be a thousand different systems of religion."

After fourteen years at Sacred Heart parish, and a few more years at two other parishes, Solanus was transferred back to St. Bonaventure Monastery in Detroit. The doorkeeper's reputation as "the holy priest" was already well known, and each day, as in New York, the steady stream of needy ones filed into his office, hoping for miracle cures for cancer, paralysis, broken limbs, troubled minds and more. And when they were healed, some on the spot, he turned away their praise, telling them, "No, praise God, *he* is the one whose love has healed you!"

During the Great Depression, the friars started a soup kitchen, which often fed up to three thousand people daily. Solanus helped, begging from the rich and poor alike, and urging visitors to help in the kitchen as a sign of their "expectant faith." Once, when there was no more bread, Solanus gathered the workers together to pray the Our Father. As they finished, a bakery truck drove up with a load of bread, so much the driver needed help unloading it. Solanus had worked his own Miracle of Loaves (no Fishes). "See," he said, "no one will starve if you put your confidence in God!"

After twenty-one years at St. Bonaventure's, Solanus was growing older and more frail, and his superiors, wanting to ease his work, sent him to a friary in Huntingdon, Indiana, for a chance to rest and enjoy the nature he had loved since he was a child. He wandered through the orchards, breathed in the fragrance of fruit blossoms and took care of the community's hives of bees. The bees fascinated him with their wonderfully complex and organized lives. And although he spent hours with them, he was never stung. Whenever the bees seemed disturbed, he played his harmonica and they settled down.

It is just as well he didn't play his violin, for his skill had not improved with age. Solanus took such a pure joy in fiddling, even though what resulted was music only to his ears. Sometimes when he played, the friars turned up the volume on the radio or simply left the room. Then he would go to the chapel and play his heart out for an admiring audience of one who was never a critic. On the Christmas Eve before Solanus died, a young friar going past the chapel heard "strange sounds" within. He peeked in and found Solanus playing the violin and singing carols to the Christ Child, perhaps remembering that first Christmas Eve so many years ago, when he first came to the chapel.

Solanus the healer was indifferent to his own ailments. He had developed a skin condition on his legs, a rash that made him scratch and scratch until the skin became raw and infected. The rashes were so bad, the doctors thought his legs would have to be amputated, but he began to improve and returned to Detroit.

Then the rash spread all over his body and the pain worsened. His poor old body, now eighty-seven years old, just seemed too weary to get better. He said to his superior, "I look upon my whole life and I want to give until there is nothing left of me to give." When it was time for him to die, he wanted with one deliberate act to "give my last breath to God."

And that is exactly what he did. On July 31, 1957, he opened his eyes and stretched forth his hands and with his final breath said, clearly, "I give my soul to Jesus Christ!"

At his funeral, thousands of people wound their way through the streets of Detroit to pay their final respects to the humble doorkeeper who welcomed them into God's love. All had different stories of how he had touched them, but they agreed as one woman cried, "he was the best friend I had in the world."

In 1995, Pope John Paul II declared Solanus, the compassionate friend, a *Venerable* friend as well.

POPE JOHN XXIII

When Angelo Guiseppe Roncalli was born, his big sisters called him Little Angelo, and he was that to them forever. When he grew up, the rest of the world called him *il buona papa*, Good Pope John XXIII.

No one would ever have imagined that this fourth child in a family of twelve children would one day grow up to be one of the most influential popes of all time. He was born on November 25, 1881, in the village of Sotto il Monte, in the province of Bergamo, Italy. He grew up in a large loving, farming family and a community where everyone knew each other as family. Angelo was a happy child, with no other plan for his life than to be a farmer, tilling the fields with his brothers.

But beneath the daily laughter and turmoil of family life, another life was growing within his soul. God spoke softly, inquiring, proposing, and Angelo listened and quietly considered. He realized that as much as he wanted to spend his days forever in Sotto il Monte, God had other plans for him, scary plans. He was to carry the Lord to the world, to serve and to love everyone by becoming a priest.

This was a big goal for a twelve-year-old, but it helped ease his sadness when he left home for the seminary in Bergamo. He was at heart a homebody, and it hurt to leave his loved ones. But Bergamo was not far away, he reasoned, and there would be visits. He hoped to become a teacher at the seminary, so that Sotto il Monte would always be within reach.

But at Bergamo, he did so well that his superiors decided he should finish his studies in Rome. Rome! The very thought overwhelmed him. But, as would become his habit, Angelo fought his fears and reluctance and embraced his new adventure. If God put him into this bustling city life, he could handle it.

Before he knew it, he was enjoying excursions to the theater, lecture halls and museums, not to mention mingling with people from all over the world. Life in Rome, he decided, was wonderful! Then the new bishop of Bergamo, who was looking for a secretary, singled out Angelo for the job. Angelo found himself on the way back to Bergamo, taking on the new work as well as resuming his studies with his usual attitude of zestful optimism.

In the journal that Angelo had begun during his early seminary years, he confided that he had "a passionate desire to study...a restless longing to know everything, to study all the great authors...new systems of thought, their continual evolution. I shall always try to introduce into discussions...a great moderation, balance, and serenity of judgment...."

He saw for himself "a mission of union and harmony," a hope which became a reality and his legacy.

The bishop became a mentor and friend to Angelo. They worked together in feeding and housing the poor, in fighting for just wages and opposing war. When the bishop died in the summer of 1914, Angelo's sorrow was deep and personal, but, as always, he kept it to himself and his journal.

No longer a secretary and now an ordained priest, Angelo became a full-time teacher and spiritual director at the seminary. Here, he thought, he would spend the rest of his life. But in May, 1915, as World War I raged throughout Europe, he put aside his life as a teacher and became a hospital orderly and chaplain on the battlefield. There he visited the wounded, heard confessions, anointed the dying and did whatever he could to lessen the horror. He wrote that he often had to "fall on my knees and cry like a baby, alone in my room," at the deaths of so many young men. He became firmly convinced that "war is, and remains the greatest evil...and he who understands the meaning of Christ...and of human and Christian brotherhood can never detest it enough."

After the war, Angelo was asked to become the national director of the Society for the Propagation of the Faith, the branch of the Vatican that oversees missionaries all over the world. Angelo didn't want this honor. For one thing, he told the director, "I am someone who doesn't get much done; by nature, lazy, I write very slowly and am easily distracted." In the end he accepted the job, because he couldn't refuse his orders. He now had the new title of monsignor.

Contrary to his fears, Angelo found enjoyment in his new work. He traveled to many countries, met a variety of people and learned about customs unknown to him. After ten years, Monsignor Roncalli was given a new assignment: Apostolic Visitor to Bulgaria. Bulgaria! It might as well have been Timbuktu for all he knew about the country. He would happily have served in any part of his sunny homeland. Why Bulgaria? Nevertheless, he obeyed his orders, and was soon named archbishop.

Bulgarians were mostly Muslims and Orthodox Christians. In order to visit the Catholics, who were a minority living in the nooks and crannies throughout the country, Angelo traveled by mule cart, raft and whatever it took to get to them.

As the years passed, Angelo believed he would spend the rest of his life working here and he didn't mind at all: "I continue to be well and live peacefully and happily, without any thought but to do the will of the Lord. I...let myself go in the arms of Providence..." But after ten years, Angelo was assigned to yet another adventure—the Apostolic Delegate to Turkey and Greece. Here the government and politics were hostile to religion in general, and there was a wall of dislike between the Catholic and Orthodox priests. But Angelo tried "to pull out a brick here and there" in this wall.

He introduced himself as a man, "like every other man on earth. I come from a particular family and place. I have been blessed with...enough common sense to grasp things quickly and clearly. I also have an inclination to love people...It stops me from doing harm to anyone; it encourages me to do good to all."

And he seized every opportunity to do just that. War had once again broken out in Europe, when Germany invaded Poland in September 1939. The Jews, who were on the Germans' list of "inferior" people to be exterminated, fled Poland to wherever they could find refuge, and Angelo used his power, money and connections to help them. He appealed to the King of Bulgaria, the Red Cross, obtained documents, clothes, vehicles and routes of escape for them. "Poor children of Israel," he wrote, "Daily I hear their groans around me. They are the relatives and countrymen of Jesus."

He is said to have saved the lives of twenty-four thousand Jews, probably more.

These experiences brought out his compassion for "our separated brethren." He exhorted Catholics not to stay within the fortress of "their own village," cutting themselves off from other faiths and nonbelievers, for "Jesus came to break the barriers; he died to proclaim universal brotherhood...."

In December of 1944, he received a telegram appointing him as Nuncio to France. Here Angelo began a new and amazing career as a diplomat. As representative of the Vatican, he gave dinner parties for the sophisticated circle of statesmen, intellectuals, artists and diplomats. Angelo, with his wit and gracious warmth, made friends with everybody. He was almost seventy now, and with age he had become more lighthearted and fearless. At receptions he would be seen with a glass of champagne in his hand, laughing and enjoying himself. Always, one journalist reported, around the archbishop there was "graceful conversation like lacework."

While he was in Paris, he became the official Vatican observer to the United Nations Educational, Scientific and Cultural Organization (UNESCO). He encouraged Catholics to "meet others without distrust...come to one another's aid without compromise." Here he saw the evidence of his conviction that war was evil and wrote down thoughts and ideas that would one day be published in his encyclical, *Pacem In Terris*—"Peace on Earth."

In 1953 when Angelo was made a cardinal, the cathedral in Paris was crammed with dignitaries of the state and church. Angelo had come to love Paris as his home and its people as his flock and hoped to stay there. But once again, God had another congregation in mind: the city of Venice, city of canals and gondolas and artists and incomparable beauty!

He spent five years here, doing "good to all," visiting every parish, working to help the poor, blessing all ventures of his parish. He even welcomed a meeting of the Socialist Party to Venice with a prayer that the congress might bridge the gap between them and the Catholics. "Isn't courtesy the first aim of charity?" he asked.

When Pope Pius XII died in October of 1958, Angelo went to Rome to help choose the new pope, never thinking that he would again have to leave a parish he had come to love. Yet, God had one more spectacular adventure for him. The voting began at the Vatican and after the eleventh ballot had been counted, and the white smoke sent swirling into the sky, a new pope emerged onto the balcony and blessed the cheering crowd: Angelo Roncalli, who would now be known as Pope John XXIII.

Listening to the news on the radio in his old home, the pope's youngest sister, Assunta, jumped up and screamed, "Oh my God, they've picked Angelino!"

Pope John's papacy was a short one, five years, but it is crammed full of stories that show his warmth and simplicity, enough for a long life's reign. In many ways he delighted in shaking up stuffy Vatican routines as no other pope had done before. Before John, the Vatican gardens were closed to the public, but John quickly cancelled the No Admittance order. "Why shouldn't others come here and look? I don't want to be ruler of a prison or cemetery." Once on a walk he surprised a group of workers who quickly dropped their tools and backed away. "Why are they doing this?" he asked his assistant. "For reasons of security," he was told. "But why?" he persisted, "I wouldn't hurt them!"

Even in his papal robes and finery, Angelo looked more like the peasant he was than a statesman. He was short and fat and bald, with a large hooked nose and huge ears. He had a carefree sense of humor about his looks. When he sat for a famous photographer, he sighed, "The Lord knew from all eternity I was going to be Pope—you'd think he would have made me more photogenic!" When he saw himself in a mirror, he chuckled and said, "Lord, this man is going to be a disaster on television!"

In keeping with his goal of welcoming and loving everyone,

Pope John called an ecumenical council, extending the hand of friendship to all Christians and others. When asked his purpose in doing this gigantic undertaking, he walked across his room in the Vatican and threw open the windows. "We intend to let in a little fresh air!" he laughed.

On the first day of this great gathering, Pope John spoke with passion to the assemblage, asking them not to listen to the prophets of doom but to Divine Providence, who "is leading us to a new view of human...relations...which are directed towards the fulfillment of God's superior and inscrutable designs...."

At the end of the day, John blessed the thousands in the courtyard below his balcony—nuns, priests, tourists, shopkeepers and more—and said with delight, "Look at them—the whole family is here!"

John knew that he was ill with cancer and probably would not live to see the end of the Council. But he still had one more adventure to complete: the writing of his encyclical, *Pacem In Terris*, which would be "for men of good will everywhere in the world." It would be a statement of the rights and responsibilities of humans in the conduct of life and the achievements of peace.

In this letter to the world, Angelo left us the legacy of his belief that "every human has the right to freedom in searching for the truth, and the right to honor God according to the dictates of an upright conscience....Every believer in this world of ours must be a spark of light, a center of love...."

Pacem In Terris was published on Holy Thursday 1963, the day Christ told his disciples to love one another. Two months later, Pope John XXIII, little Angelino, spark of light, died. His last words were "Christ died for all, for all. No one is excluded from his love...."

TERESA BENEDICTA OF THE CROSS (EDITH STEIN)

Edith Stein's story is like the story of Easter—eventually triumphant, but very sad in the making. It was a life of misunderstanding, rejection, setbacks, unfulfillment and ultimately martyrdom, laced together with suffering. By human standards, her life and death was a tragic loss. But God took those broken fragments of failures and her tragic death and created a masterpiece of stark beauty.

Edith was born in Breslau, Germany, the eleventh child of an Orthodox Jewish family, on October 12, 1891, which happened to be Yom Kippur, the Day of Atonement. Her father died when she was two years old, leaving her mother to raise the family and manage the family lumberyard on her own. Edith and her mother had a strong, loving bond, but that love was tested when Edith, at the age of thirteen, decided she didn't believe in God or her faith anymore.

Her mother thought it was probably the rebellion of a feisty, independent teenager and prayed it would pass. But it didn't. Edith went away to college, a happy atheist, at the University of Gottingen, where she eagerly plunged into the study of philosophy. Her brilliant mind blossomed and was encouraged by a circle of student friends and professors. But World War I soon interrupted university life, and she volunteered for nursing duty. Some of her closet friends had died at the front, among them one of her professors, Adolf Reinach. She visited his widow to comfort her but instead was consoled by her and her Christian faith. She wondered if perhaps she had been wrong in thinking religion was a waste of time.

After the war, she went with her professor, Edmund Husserl, as his assistant to the University of Frieberg and, at the age of twenty-three, finished her dissertation. She was now, officially, a Doctor of Philosophy, and her future as scholar and teacher seemed assured.

It was around this time that she picked up Saint Teresa of Avila's autobiography. She read it in one night, unable to stop. When she closed the book, she declared, "This is the truth." Edith was first and foremost a truth-seeker. She discovered the truth she had been seeking not in the works of philosophers but in the story of another woman of Jewish ancestry. It led her to the certainty that "Truth is not found in a system of ideas but in a Person—a Person on the Cross."

She was baptized a Catholic on New Year's Day 1922. Her mother was heartbroken and wept bitterly, and many of her Jewish friends cut off all ties with her. For the next nine years, she taught at colleges in Speyer and Munster, but the Nazi party was coming into power and trying to rid the country of Jews. Edith's career as a teacher came to an end because doors were closing to Jews at the universities.

She had a foreboding of worse things ahead, so she wrote to Pope Pius XI, alerting him to what was going on and asking for a private audience. But her letter was never answered. In October 1933, Edith had decided that her true vocation was to become a Carmelite nun, so she applied to the convent in Cologne. Once again her mother was upset and angrily charged that she was abandoning her people to join their persecutors. None of her family was present when she was clothed in the Carmelite habit on April 15, 1934.

Edith took for her name *Teresa Benedicta a Croce*—"Teresa Blessed by the Cross" or "Teresa Benedicta of the Cross"—a name chosen to honor the foundress of her order and to refer "to the fate of the people of God, which even then was beginning to reveal itself." She wrote, "I spoke with the Savior to tell him I realized it was his Cross that was now being laid upon the Jewish people, and that the few who understood this had the responsibility of carrying it in the name of all, and that I myself was willing to do this, if he would only show me how."

More and more, as conditions worsened in Germany, she was drawn into what she called the Science of the Cross, "the mystery of suffering, of victory in failure, of dying and rising in Christ...to walk on the dirty and rough paths of this earth and yet to be enthroned with Christ...to laugh and cry with the children of this world and ceaselessly sing the praises of God with the choirs of angels—this is the life of the Christian until the morning of eternity breaks forth."

In November 1938, all-out war against the Jews began, and Edith began her own rough path. She allowed herself to be smuggled out of the country to a Carmelite convent in Echt, Holland, not to escape the fate of her people, but rather to spare her sisters from any reprisals for harboring a Jew. She had already written a prayer offering herself to the heart of Jesus as a sacrifice for the Jewish people, for the aversion of war and for the sanctification of her Carmel family. She was prepared for whatever awaited her.

Edith resumed her normal convent life in Echt, working on a book about Saint John of the Cross, until the Nazis invaded and occupied Holland in 1940. She was not bothered because the Nazis had promised to spare the Jewish-Christians, provided there was no criticism of the Germans by the church. When, in July 1942, a statement of the Catholic Bishops denouncing the persecution of the Jews was read from the pulpits, the infuriated Nazis retaliated by placing all Jewish Christians under arrest.

On the Sunday afternoon of August 2, while Edith was absorbed in her writing, the German officers came and took Edith and Rosa, her sister, who had been living at the convent. As they were being led away, Edith put her arm around Rosa, who was quite frightened and comforted her, "Come Rosa, we are going for our people."

They went, with thousands of other Jews, first to a camp in northern Holland, Westerbork, where she is remembered for her composure and gentle consoling of other women, and her caring for the little ones, washing them, combing their hair and making sure they were fed. On August 7, they and others were deported to Auschwitz, where they died in the gas chamber on August 9, 1942.

Fifty years later, Edith was canonized by Pope John Paul II as Saint Teresa Benedicta, saint and martyr of the church. In his homily, the pope said,

> In the years that she studied... God did not play an important part, at least initially. Her thinking was based on a demanding ethical idealism... she did not want to accept anything without careful examination, not even the faith of her fathers. She wanted to get to the bottom of things herself.... "My search for truth," she said, "is itself a very profound sense a search for God." Let us open ourselves for her message to us as a woman of the spirit and of the mind, who saw in the Science of the Cross the acme of all

wisdom. May the new saint be an example to us in our commitment to serve freedom, in our search for the truth. May her witness constantly strengthen the bridge of mutual understanding between Jews and Christians.

MAXIMILIAN KOLBE

We are all called to be saints, but some of us have more of a struggle to get there than others. Some are pushed, shoved, practically dragged against their wills into holiness. Some of us, even with the best of intentions and God's grace, stumble, trip, fall flat on our faces, get up and do it all over again. And some, a very few, come to earth with holiness bred into the bone. They could not be other than a saint. One of these few was Maximilian Kolbe.

He was born Raymond, the second of Julius and Maria Kolbe's five sons, in the village of Zdunska Wola, Poland. His parents were weavers, and although they did make ends meet, they were not well-to-do; neither were any of their neighbors. Poland did not exist as a country after World War I; it had been divided up and given to Austria, Prussia and Russia. The Kolbes lived in the part under Russian rule, but they and all their friends stubbornly and secretly clung to their Polish tradition and religion.

Raymond, a cheerful, happy-go-lucky child, had a special love for our Lady. Before he was seven years old, he had an experience with her that set the course of his life. He had been scolded by his mother for some tomfoolery. "What's to become of you, when you carry on like that?" she snapped. He became very silent, and then went behind the curtain that hid their family shrine to Mary.

For the next few days, he was serious, unsmiling, and his mother was worried. "What's wrong, son?" she asked. "Tell me the truth. You know you must tell Mama everything."

Tearfully he explained, "I prayed to our Lady to tell me what *would* become of me, and she came to me holding a crown in each hand, one white and one red. She asked me which one I would like—white meant I would remain pure, and red that I would be a martyr. I said I wanted them both. Then she smiled at me and left...." He told this only to his mother, and they kept the secret between them.

When he was thirteen, Raymond and his older brother, Francis, crossed over the border into Austrian territory to enter a Franciscan seminary for teenage boys. With his never-ending curiosity about how things work, he eagerly delved into the mysteries of math and physics and soon became an honor student.

He played chess and soccer with equal passion, and he was fascinated with science fiction. He diagrammed models for rockets, planned interplanetary flight and a high velocity vehicle to take photographs in outer space, and he wanted to invent a time machine that would pick up sound waves from the past so they could hear the voice of Jesus. If he had lived in our age of television, he probably would have been a fan of *Star Trek*!

He also had a gift for military strategy and planning

fortifications, and he truly loved the idea of being a soldier. Drawing on his love for Mary, he decided that he wanted to be a soldier for Mary and could do this best by entering the military. He even convinced his brother to come with him. They were on their way to tell the rector of their decision, when they bumped into their mother, who had come for a visit. No one knows what she said (but we can imagine) when they told her their plans. All we know is that they changed their minds and continued on their paths to the priesthood.

After two years in the novitiate, Raymond went to Rome to study further. It was during the next six years that the lively young man with the unstoppable imagination got the idea to form an army that would fight for God through Mary. He called it the *Militia Immaculatae*, the Knights of Mary, and Mary was the *Immaculata*.

When he was in Rome, he took the name Maximilian—Max to his friends. In the official book of comings and goings, the lector of the college inscribed: "Maximilian Kolbe, province of Galicia, arrived 10/29/1912, ordained to priesthood, April 28, 1918. A young saint."

His first assignment was to teach in a seminary at Cracow, and here he began to recruit members for the Militia Immaculatae among members of his order, professors and students, to begin with. The membership was growing by leaps and bounds when Maximilian had an attack of tuberculosis, the illness that would be with him all his life. When it got very bad, he would leave his work to go to a sanatorium, where rest, fresh air and good food would heal him temporarily, but he was never free of tuberculosis. Even while sick, he took every opportunity to tell others about Christ and Mary, never pushing or forcing, but always willing—night or day—to answer questions and share his beliefs.

His next idea was to publish a magazine dedicated to Mary. When he asked permission of his superior to do this, he got it, with the understanding that he would have to raise the money himself. Maximilian's enthusiasm in believing completely in providence to supply all that was needed was sometimes considered foolish and impractical, even among members of his own order. But nothing could dissuade him when he felt he must do the will of God, and providence always came through!

He begged enough money to publish the first *Knight of the Immaculata*, which he gave away on the streets. After a few more issues, he ran out of money, so he went to pray for reinforcements from Mary. He noticed a sack on the altar so he investigated and read the note pinned to it: "for my dear mother, Mary Immaculate." Inside was the exact amount of money he needed.

Then a visiting priest gave him one hundred dollars, which he used to buy an ancient, hand-operated printing press. He, the press and several brothers were allowed to move to a friary in Grodno, where there would be more room for his work. He and another brother kept down expenses by sharing one coat and a pair of shoes. When one went out, the other stayed in. It's a good thing they never had to go out together!

Young men who had read the *Knight* began showing up, not only to be priests but also to work in the new publishing apostolate. Within five years, they had outgrown their space, so Maximilian hunted for the right spot on which to build a bigger, better friary. He found it, just outside Warsaw, but it was owned by a Polish prince who was asking more money for it than Maximilian had. Nevertheless, Maximilian met with the prince, who was impressed with the humble friar and his dreams of a "city of Mary." He said to Maximilian, "No, you cannot buy this land. It is too expensive. So I give it to you!"

And here the City of Mary—Niepokalanow—was built. The first night, they put some wooden planks across their suitcases, seeing as there was no building, sat on the ground and ate the food the villagers had brought. Providence had provided! Then, with volunteers—Catholics, Jews, whomever—the friars built a shack to live in and a small chapel.

Within three years, it had come to resemble a small city, with many buildings, craft shops, a printery and a seminary for the many young men who answered their calls to work for Mary. The old press had been replaced by modern machines that put 400,000 copies of the magazine into circulation.

Maximilian believed there was good in every*thing* as well as every person. He was very much a practical man of this world, and his theme was "study everything, from Communism to show business, and build on what is good in it." For example, while many frowned on the movies as an "evil tool" and were trying to suppress them, he disagreed. "The movie was meant to benefit society. Our job is to get it moving in that direction." A shocked friend said, "How can you say such a thing? Don't you know the devil always takes over new inventions?" To which Maximilian replied, "Then that's all the more reason for us to finally wake up and get to work! If Jesus or Saint Francis were alive today, they would use modern technology to reach the people!"

He kept up to date on all communist and atheistic literature, believed Christians should not condemn communism without knowing what was good in it. Some years later, a communist who visited Niepokalanow told him, "This is the real communism, right here, the way you're living!"

He also believed that no one should take on extra penances, fasts, chains, kneeling for hours on stone floors, or that sort of thing. "It's enough penance to fulfill the will of the Immaculata" by accepting the challenges and opportunities God gives us each day. He insisted on good, plain nourishing food for his friars, and on no smoking, not only because it was bad for one's health but also because it set a bad example.

After three years, in 1930, Maximilian surprised his superior with a request to go to Japan to build another City of Mary there. "Why Japan?" asked the surprised priest, "when things are going so well in Poland?" "Because the Blessed Mother has her plan ready," smiled Maximilian.

He argued so persuasively that the superior agreed, reluctantly, but said that Maximilian must finance the trip himself. "Don't worry," smiled Maximilian. "I have my benefactors." And indeed, in no time he and four of his brothers had packed their bags and were off on a steamer bound for the Orient. (On the way, they visited the shrines of two of his "benefactors"—Saint Bernadette of Lourdes and Saint Thérèse of Lisieux.)

After they landed in Nagasaki, Japan, the first thing they had to do was learn the language so they could set the type to publish a newspaper the people could understand. (Hardly any Japanese could read Polish.) Within a month, they were on the streets giving away two thousand copies of *The Knight* in the native language, always bowing politely and exchanging cards so they would not offend the Japanese, to whom manners were very important.

Their life in Japan was another daring adventure of trust, so much so that the bishop of Nagasaki said disapprovingly, "They have taken the idea of trusting in Divine Providence to the point of abuse!" It did look that way. They had no furniture, slept on the floor, cooked outdoors with only a metal sheet overhead to keep rain and snow off the food.

The food itself must have been a true penance to those Polish friars who loved their meat and potatoes and *pierogies*! Instead they ate the food of the country—strange green vegetables, fish, rice, tea. The weather was harsh and unrelentingly cold. In a letter home, Maximilian wrote: "Heavy snow fell in the night. To sleep we had to cover our heads as the snow was hitting our faces. In the morning our dormitory was absolutely white and the basins full of ice!"

Soon they were able to buy land for their home, which they called the Garden of Mary. It was cheap, on steep, hilly land—a foolish venture, said practical people. But they kept on building. In the end, Maximilian's choice proved providential when the atomic bomb leveled the city of Nagasaki at the end of World War II, and the Garden proved the only safe haven for thousands of refugee children.

The friars won over the Japanese, who have a love of heroic bravery and total dedication to a noble cause. Maximilian, in return, loved and respected them. Never in his life did he distinguish among people. He saw Christ in every one of them, and that was sufficient. As much as he yearned for them to come to know Mary and God as he did, he knew they must choose this way of life freely.

After six years in Japan, Maximilian was ready to go on, dreaming of building his next center in India. But when he learned he had been elected superior, he knew he must return to Niepokalanow. Ever obedient, he said his goodbyes, packed his bags and went back to Poland again threatened by war, this time from its neighbor Germany.

When the Germans did invade Poland in September 1939, the Poles resisted bravely but were crushed. It was not long before Maximilian and his friars were arrested as political prisoners and spent the time between September and December in detention camps. Here Maximilian's holiness shone bright and clear, as he tenderly cared for his fellow prisoners, calming and comforting them, lifting their spirits with prayers and songs. Even a few German guards respected him and got him extra food (which he gave away) because he was ill.

On the day Maximilian was set free, December 8, the Feast of the Immaculate Conception, he shook hands with one guard warmly and invited him to visit Niepokalanow anytime.

After he returned to the friary, he wrote a thank-you note to another guard's mother, saying, "When I was interned...I had the good luck to meet your son. All of us, dear lady, were struck by his high degree of culture and his profound sense of justice." Maximilian did not know the meaning of the word *enemy*.

At Niepokalanow, he found the monastery almost demolished, the printing presses smashed or carried off, the statues of Mary broken. But he rallied all the brothers around and they began at once to clean up the mess. They set up shops that would be of use to the community—bicycle and farm machine repair, a dairy, a cobbler shop, for which the Germans provided oil and iron, since it benefited them too.

And they took care of all refugees, as many as fifteen hundred at a time. As Jesus fed the crowds with loaves and fishes, so too Maximilian and his brothers gave food, housing, clothes, medicine, whatever was needed to their guests.

Maximilian had heard news about the dreaded concentration camps, where the Germans had collected the "undesirables"—Jews, gypsies, political prisoners (priests, nuns, professors, any who dared to protest the war). They were brought here supposedly to work and support the war effort, but the sad truth was that none were ever meant to leave the camps alive.

Many innocent people whose "crime" was to be of the wrong race or religion were treated as less than human, even less than animals. Women and children and those too sick to be of use were put to death in gas chambers. Those who were strong and fit were worked and abused until they too died on their own or were shot while trying to escape.

Maximilian wondered how long it would before they came for him and his brothers. He was sure it would happen, for he was well-known as the editor of *The Knight*, which would make him an enemy of the state. And it did happen. He and four other priests at the friary were sent to the camp at Auschwitz in May 1941.

It would be hard to find a place more unlikely to preach or believe in the goodness of Christ and Mary, but Maximilian did it. Only God knows how many souls he saved from despair with his tender words and care. He secretly heard confessions and gave Communion from his daily portion of bread. He gave them everything he had, and finally, he gave himself.

On a hot summer afternoon near the end of July, the prison siren blared, signaling a prisoner's escape. The men of Cell Block 14, the prisoner's cell, were terrified, for they knew the price they would pay. All six hundred men, including Maximilian, lined up in precise rows, while the commander walked up and down, picking out a man here, a man there, prolonging the ordeal with cruel enjoyment, until he had fingered ten men. They would be taken to the starvation bunker to die, in payment for the prisoner who had escaped. Starvation was a cruel way to die, often taking two weeks before the last painful death was drawn.

One of the men began to sob. "Please, I have a wife and children," he cried brokenly. The soldiers laughed and pushed him roughly with their guns. Quietly, a small man stepped out of line and walked down the row to within sight of the commander. "I wish to make a request, please," he said in German.

No one made a sound. Shock filled the air. The commander was too surprised to shoot him on the spot. "What do you want?" he snapped.

"I would like to take the place of the prisoner. I have not wife or children. Besides, I'm old. He's in better condition to work than I am."

"Who are you?" shouted the commander, growing uneasy.

"A Catholic priest."

The commander, wanting to close the matter quickly, said, "Request granted."

And so the men marched to the bunker, to their certain death, Maximilian staggering under the weight of another, too grief-stricken to walk under his own strength.

Two weeks later, Max was the only one still alive in the dark, dank death-chamber, and the commander ordered him to be injected with carbolic acid, which would cause almost instant death. His body, along with his nine comrades, was burned in the crematorium the next morning, August 15, 1941.

Many years before, he said, "I would like to be ground to dust for the Immaculate Virgin and have this dust be blown away by the wind all over the world."

And so, on the morning of the Feast of the Assumption of Mary, the ashes of Maximilian Kolbe blew away to every corner of the world. And on October 10, 1982, the gentle man who yearned to love without limits, was consecrated saint by his countryman, Pope John Paul II.

CATHOLIC WORKER
THE

Vol CX No 4   June-July   Price 1¢

Study
War No
More

Power
In
Non-Vio

DOROTHY DAY

Sometimes we think of saints as holy "faraway" people who lived long ago in castles or convents. Oh, they must have had problems with wars and plagues and persecution, but these were *nothing* like our problems: speeding cars or terrorists or poisoned streams or atomic bombs or the awful things we live with today.

But one woman, whom many call a saint, knew all the fears we do and the injustices and did something about them. Her name was Dorothy Day.

Dorothy was born in Brooklyn, New York, in 1897. Her father, a journalist, moved the family to California when he became sports editor of the San Francisco newspaper. When the great earthquake of 1906 destroyed their home, he found another reporting job in Chicago, where the family put down new roots in a very different life.

City life, with its rows of tenements jammed with noisy families, startled eight-year-old Dorothy at first, but soon she got used to the chaos and made new friends. Two of them were from large Irish Catholic families. They showed a strong, loyal love for one another, despite the usual bickering, and there was always a real baby to play with instead of a doll. Mary Harrington, one friend, told her stories of saints such as Thérèse and Joseph, and Dorothy tucked them away into her heart. What an incredible way to spend one's life, she thought, loving God as these saints did!

Dorothy's family was Episcopalian, but they no longer practiced their religion. As she grew older, it meant less and less to her. She thought all religion made people lazy and too accepting of evil. "They only believe they'll find happiness in heaven, so why bother about earth?" is what she thought about religious people, and she shook her head over their foolishness.

She put all her energy into learning about the world. She read everything—her mind was like a computer, gobbling up facts and storing them for future use. She loved the books written by the great Russian writers and philosophers and felt a kindred spirit to them and to the new communist revolution.

Dorothy didn't believe in waiting for heavenly happiness. She couldn't bear to see mothers and children suffering and fathers working for unjust wages. When she received a scholarship to college, she vowed to use her knowledge to make the world better. She would write words to stir people's souls and open their eyes to injustice, and she would do it all without God's help—if there *was* a God!

Then her father changed jobs, and the family moved to New

York City, and Dorothy quit school to join them. She got a job on *The New York Call* and then on *The Masses*, both papers published for the working people. She covered strikes, picketing and the peace movement, and she got to know firsthand the workers' problems.

Dorothy and her father quarreled over her strong beliefs, and she left home. The newspapers closed down, and Dorothy, jobless, joined a group of women going to Washington, D.C., to demand the right to vote. They carried banners as they marched past the White House, and people along the way jeered at them.

Dorothy and thirty-four other women were arrested and jailed for thirty days. When she was released, she said she never again would be free as long as there were others suffering in prisons.

She wrote a novel, which she sold to a Hollywood movie company for five thousand dollars, a huge sum in those days. She felt like a millionaire! Dorothy bought a cottage on Staten Island, New York, a lovely refuge, she said, with solitude to write. She met a man with whom she fell deeply in love, and he came to live with her at the cottage.

When she learned she was to have a baby, she was so thrilled and grateful for the new life within her, she even thanked the God she once thought didn't exist. She asked God to enter her life. As he gradually did, she began to see that Christ and his gospel were the true answer to the world's problems.

When her daughter, Tamar Teresa, was born, Dorothy had her baptized as a Catholic. Tamar's father was furious and told Dorothy she would have to choose between him and God. She did. From that moment, she became a single mother with a child to raise.

Dorothy became a Catholic a few months later. She wondered what work she could do now, what use she could make of her talent. How would she care for Tamar? She knelt in a darkened church pew and asked God to show her the way.

She came home to find a short, stocky, weather-beaten man with a warm smile awaiting her. He told her, in a thick French accent, that he was Peter Maurin, and he wanted to talk to her about ways to help the poor and give them dignity and equality. He wanted to open what he called Houses of Hospitality for them where none would be turned away. He said the Lord would provide all that was necessary.

Dorothy listened, fascinated. She was sure this little man was sent from heaven! "The first thing we must do," Peter continued, without waiting for her response, "is start a newspaper, put down what we need to do for a better life. We will write about war and peace and food and shelter and scholars and artists—all of us who make up the Mystical Body of Christ!"

And so, on May 1, 1933, *The Catholic Worker* was born. Peter and Dorothy had saved $57 to print 2,500 copies of the paper, which they sold in the streets for a penny a copy. Then they opened the first House of Hospitality in New York City. Dorothy called upon her old friends, Joseph and Thérèse, to help meet their needs and bills, and the saints always obliged!

Dorothy traveled about the country, encouraging others to open Houses of Hospitality, and soon new houses were sprouting up in Boston and Chicago and Philadelphia. Then she and Peter began Catholic Worker farms, where families could grow their own food and raise their children by the laws of God and nature.

It wasn't an easy life for Dorothy. It is never easy being misunderstood. She was often condemned for putting the gospel into social action. She was called a communist traitor for protesting war and violence. She often marched with strikers and went to jail with them.

"I don't care what people think of me," she said. "There is only one judge who really matters."

Dorothy died at the age of eighty-three. She had given her life in service to God's poor—the helpless and the hopeless. Besides the example of her life, she left us *The Catholic Worker*, still a penny a copy and her words to encourage us:

> God doesn't expect us to succeed...all he asks is that we hang in there, bearing witness, loving, sharing ourselves with those who have no one else...and we can only do it with his help.

CARYLL HOUSELANDER

When you think of an eccentric person, what comes to mind? A neighbor who *must* pull her shades down exactly thirteen and a half inches from the top? An old lady who lives alone with seven cats? The teenager around the corner who wears one red shoe and one black shoe? People who pay their bills in dimes?

Everyone knows someone who seems a little off-center, who lives in a way that seems strange or silly to us. But we should remember that eccentrics hide holiness well. They dance to a heavenly piper, and it really doesn't matter to them that they are performing solo. The only audience they aim to please is God.

One of these "divine eccentrics" was Caryll Houselander. She was born October 29, 1901, to Gertrude and Wilmot Houselander in Bath, England. From the moment of her birth, Caryll lived an unconventional life.

She was so odd-looking, "like a tiny red fish," and seemed not to want to stay in the world. When the minister asked what her name would be (her uncle had summoned him quickly because she was so frail), her mother and uncle began to giggle—they hadn't thought of any. Finally they decided on the name of a yacht her mother had sailed on, the *Caryll*, and baptized her, with a salad bowl as the font.

After such a beginning, you would think things had to get better, but they didn't. All her life Caryll had poor health and was afflicted with mysterious (and known) diseases, crippling discomforts and aches from head to toe. No sooner did she recover from one disease than her body broke down with another.

She also suffered emotionally. Her childhood was not happy. "I was not only an unwanted child but an unnatural one," she tells us, "and I took an immediate dislike to my unfortunate mother." They had little in common. Her mother loved hunting and all sports, which Caryll loathed. Says a friend of the family, "Gert was as hard as nails; hard and loud, game for anything. She was not deliberately unkind, but she stomped on Caryll's feelings."

Her mother converted to Catholicism, and at the age of six, Caryll and her sister, Ruth, also became Catholics. Shortly after Caryll's ninth birthday, their parents separated, and the two girls went to board at the Convent of the Holy Child Jesus outside Birmingham.

Caryll's emotional wounds began to heal with the affection of the French nuns and "the beauty of austerity...the simplicity of having only what is essential, which is balm to the troubled mind...."

Here she had her first glimpse of the suffering Christ. England was in the midst of the First World War, and even in the convent, the English and French nuns had strong feelings against the Germans. Caryll would often help a Bavarian lay sister who knew no English and had no friends, because she felt sorry for her. One evening she had been polishing shoes when Caryll arrived. She writes:

When I had come quite close to her...I saw that she was
weeping; tears were running down her rosy cheeks and
falling onto the blue apron and the child's shoes.....I saw
her large, toilworn hands come down onto her lap and fold
on the little shoes, and those hands, red and chapped, with
blunted nails, were folded in a way that expressed
inconsolable grief....We were both...silent, I staring down
at her beautiful hands, afraid to look up, not knowing what
to say; she weeping soundlessly....At last...I raised my
head, and then—I saw—the nun was crowned with the
crown of thorns. I shall not attempt to explain this. I am
simply telling the thing as I saw it....Finding my tongue, I
said to her, "I would not cry if I was wearing the crown of
thorns like you are." ...I sat down beside her, and together
we polished the shoes. (*Rocking Horse Catholic*, pp. 73–74)

When Caryll was fifteen, she became sick at school and was
sent to live with her mother, who had moved to London. She
had her appendix removed and went to a boarding school by
the ocean to recuperate. Since she couldn't attend classes, she
grew bored and wrote a family friend for train fare to come
home. When she got it, she wrote a polite farewell note to the
headmistress and left. That was the end of her formal
schooling.

She tried to help her mother, who now ran a boardinghouse,
but she was terrible at making beds and washing dishes (she
often left pots and pans in the oven rather than clean them).
What she really wanted to do, she decided, was become an
artist, and she was able to do this when she won a scholarship
to St. John's Wood Art School.

Here she threw herself into discovering her gifts for
painting, designing and woodcarving, and here, for the first
time, she enjoyed the pleasure of making friends.

They did not seem to mind her appearance, which has been
described, kindly, as "elfin," and, not so nicely, as "grotesque."

She was "a little carroty thing," plump, short, with long red-gold hair cut in a fringe around her face and done up in a bun in the back. Her skin was very pink and she covered it with white powder, which often made her look like a clown.

To add to her income and keep herself in art supplies, she tried all kinds of jobs to earn her living—she painted lampshades, made artificial roses, decorated houses, illustrated newspaper ads for hats, corsets and powdered eggs (eventually the advertising firm went bankrupt and paid her off in chocolates!). She looked after ten children while their widowed and divorced mothers went off in search of husbands. And once she was a cleaning lady, a job that didn't last long because of her terror of mice. She couldn't bear to take the dead mice out of traps and so bribed the cooks to do it. When the bribes began to equal her salary, she quit!

All this while she clung to the Mass as the truth and beauty in her life, although her experiences with snobbish and narrow-minded Catholics often made her wonder why she was in church. One Sunday morning she arrived at Mass too late for a "free" seat ("seat money" was collected at the door for better seats). She took a place in another section, where she was confronted by an usher telling her to pay or leave. When she replied she hadn't any money, he again insisted she leave.

Caryll, red-faced and embarrassed, left that church, left the Catholic church entirely, and didn't come back for years.

Caryll began seeking other paths to God. She went to Protestant, Jewish, Buddhist and Russian Orthodox services—she was especially drawn to Russian art and spirituality. But after all the searching, she realized "I was no nearer to what I was seeking. Every creed... had something in it of truth and beauty, but it was always something that... I knew was included in the Catholic church.... Frankly, I did not *want* to be a Catholic.... What I did want, and with increasing longing, was to join the Russian church."

This yearning led her to became part of a circle of exiles from Russia who had fled the revolution and settled in England. Through them, she met Sydney Reilly, a master spy for England. They began a love affair which lasted two years. Eventually it ended, and Sydney Reilly married another woman.

She never wrote or spoke of these years, but twenty years later, she wrote to a young friend, "I know what it can feel like to part from a man whom one is in love with, for I too have done so...and the years have not lessened or dimmed the love, even though he is dead now, shot in Russia....Because I loved that man I have loved many other people, animals and things...."

Among those people was her friend, Iris Wyndam, with whom she lived until the end of her life. To help with expenses, she began carving wooden statues of Christ, Mary and "the Bambino," for churches and friends. She loved to work with wood and said that *all* wood was alive, that she could see shapes in the wood and it was her job to release them.

Soon she turned from "carving wood to shaping language." She had begun to write children's stories for a Catholic magazine and poetry, which she called "rhythms." Her theme in all her writing, as well as in her life, was the experience of Christ in daily life.

Caryll was always plagued by not having enough money. She said it was strange that "God has put into my heart the hatred of money and yet made it my duty to struggle so hard for it!" She felt a keen kinship with the poor and helpless, and with her friends wondered how they could help them, especially those "hidden poor," who kept their poverty to themselves.

They had two problems: how to get the money and how to give it. Caryll had by now returned to the Church and was immersed in the gospel. She remembered the story of the loaves and fishes and said, "Let's put down a penny each. If God wants us to do something, he will multiply it."

At that moment, a friend came into the room and saw the coins. "Whatever are those for?" he asked, and without waiting for an answer, he added, "Here, I'll multiply them," and put down five shillings.

With this sign, they decided to form the Society of Loaves and Fishes. Theirs would be a secret work, and the money (when they got it) would be given anonymously to "those faced with dire poverty...and who feel constrained to keep the fact secret." The chairman would be known as the Red Herring, the workers were Sprats and the donors were the Mackerels!

When she was twenty-seven, Caryll became a member of the Third Order of Saint Francis. "Imagine," she joked to a friend, "a Franciscan who doesn't like mice!" But she did love cats, particularly one who came to her and Iris, a small tabby cat she named Jones. They were inseparable friends for twenty years, and he was as dear to her as a human friend. Often as she worked on her books and letters late into the night, Jones would whisk his tail across the paper, "sitting on my letter, pushing the pen," trying to make her stop so she would go to bed.

In 1939 World War II began between England and Germany, and Caryll, like the rest of England, plunged into working for her country. At first she was a First Aid volunteer in the hospitals. Then she joined the Censorship Office, checking letters going out and coming into the country.

She prayed for the letter-writers, saying "I begin to imagine what it must be like to be a saint in heaven and to see all the pitiful prayers of the world passing through one's hands to God....I can pray for each one, taking the hope or grief or anxiety of each and offering it to God."

Refugees began pouring into England, and Caryll and Iris took in a group of Belgian children. An air-raid shelter was built in their garden (on top of which they grew daffodils). When a bomb fell nearby and blew out their doors and windows, the only casualty was Jones. He couldn't be found, and Caryll feared the worst. They eventually discovered him, sleeping unconcernedly inside the bomb shelter!

Caryll also watched at night for fires from the tops of buildings and worked inside the air-raid shelters when London was bombed. She began work on her first book, *This War Is the Passion*, which she wrote mostly sitting on the toilet during the night, because that was the only space and time she had.

She wrote in this book that "only an understanding of the Passion of Christ could encourage physical and spiritual survival," and that one must change one's attitude toward the enemy, even when hatred seemed justified. "There must be a genuine love for the enemy and a desire for his redemption.... We have to stretch Christ in us...to fit the size of this war... the arms of Christ stretched on the cross are the widest reach there is, the only one that encircles the whole world."

When the book was published it was such a financial success that Caryll no longer had to worry about meeting the bills. She was filled with plans for new ventures after the war—she wanted to open a bookstore in London, a home for murderesses to help them back into the community and a home for children with emotional problems.

Most of all, she wanted to keep on writing books and now letters to all who were writing her for advice and comfort. "My writing is both my life and my living," she said. "I am certain for me that the real *communion* with people is in writing." Her fame as a writer of spiritual books soon brought her a correspondence with people from all over the world, and she answered every letter, never hurried or slapdash, always understanding.

Caryll could be so compassionate about others' weaknesses because she was so well aware of her own. For all her generosity and love, she could be biting and sarcastic with those she thought arrogant and selfish. At parties she was a great mimic and made merciless fun of her victims. Then she would cry in remorse the next day and pray to Saint Peter, "Dear Saint of Impulses, pray for me that I may stop cutting off people's ears!"

In her letters she reminded her correspondents that prayer should be easy, a joy, "a simple desire to be with him," and she advised those who weren't sure how to ask for something "just to say...'Sacred Heart of Jesus, I put *all* my trust in you,' and mean it, put Our Lord on His honour...just kneel down...and put it before Him...like the old peasant who had a bad foot, but since he did not know what was best for him, to be cured, to be lame, to be in pain or out of pain, he just went to church and said, "Lord—foot!"

By 1949, Caryll was in bad physical shape. Her poor body, always inclined to catching some stray bug, combined with years of lack of sleep, improper eating and chain smoking, worked against any kind of healing. Now she was diagnosed with cancer and she would have to be operated on for its removal.

The day before the operation she wrote, "Somehow or other this all fits into God's plan....It is not for me to say 'I must live' or 'I must die'...but simply, with Christ, 'Into Thy Hands'....It is a test...to compel me, the half-trusting, to trust completely."

And, as always, she did. The cancer was removed and Caryll hoped for another chance at life. But a short time after, the cancer returned and spread. In the presence of a priest and dear friends, Caryll died on October 12, 1954.

Caryll had said about heaven, "Of the next life I have no imagination, it is something I never think of. Here on earth

Christ is almost visible, and because he is in us and with us, I agree with St. Catherine that 'all the way to heaven is heaven.'"

Yet, as the end of her life drew near, she must have wondered a little at what was to come. As she wrote in one of her poems:

Though death walks at my heels,
…this is the beginning,
not the end of my story.
I walk among the shadows,
O Liege God,
my love,
Shadows
of your bright glory!

How exciting it must have been, when she reached heaven, to come out of the shadows into her own unique glory!

MOTHER TERESA OF CALCUTTA

Whenever you hear people say, "There's so much trouble and sadness in the world, so much poverty and war and famine, I wish I could do something about it, but I'm only one person. One person can't do anything," don't believe them!

True, one person alone can do little, but one person with God can do *anything*! This is the story of such a person, a young girl named Agnes, who wanted to encircle the world with love and service for Christ. We know her today as Mother Teresa of Calcutta.

She has become such a well-known, familiar figure, we may think of her as always having been this way—a small, gentle woman, stooped with age, wearing a white sari bordered in blue, cuddling an orphaned baby or speaking at dinners in her honor, accepting awards, being the subject of television documentaries. We may not see the real person beneath the image, the humble, determined, passionate woman whose life was witness that surrender to God's will and absolute trust in his providence have made her work possible.

To see Mother Teresa as this real person, we must go back many years and imagine her as a lively, outgoing little girl named Agnes Bojaxhiu, who was born in the Yugoslavian village of Skopje in 1910. Her family life—she had a brother and sister—was happy and loving. Her parents came from the tough, proud hill people, people who were proud to be revolutionaries. If things stood in your way, you changed them or ignored them or stubbornly persevered through them.

When she was fourteen, she read in the local Sodality paper about the missionary work of the Irish nuns of Loretto working in Calcutta, and she knew without hesitation that this was the work for her. She had no doubts, even at that early age, that she would turn her life over to God, but she was reluctant to leave her family. At seventeen, she knew she could wait no longer and applied for admission to the Dublin motherhouse of the Sisters of Loretto and was accepted. She left for Ireland, sad at closing one chapter of her life, but excited at the new one she was about to begin.

After a year in Dublin, she sailed for Calcutta and the novitiate, and in two years she made her final profession. She was now Sister Teresa, named for Thérèse, the "little flower," who had yearned to be a missionary. She began teaching at a high school for middle-class Bengali girls. She stayed there for twenty years, eventually becoming headmistress, and was quite content devoting herself to the intellectual and spiritual education of these privileged students.

When they went out on weekly visits to hospitals and passed by the impoverished inhabitants of slums, Teresa yearned to help them, comfort them, but she knew that her present work would not allow her this freedom.

One day, while she was riding on a train going from Calcutta to a retreat in Darjeeling where she hoped to resolve these new questionings, she received what she called "a call within a call." It was a clear, distinct message from the Lord which told her to leave her convent to work and live among the poor. "It was an order," she says. "I knew now where I belonged, but I did not know how to get there."

She was to leave the safety and security of the convent. She was to work and serve "the poorest of the poor," the unwanted, the uncared for, homeless, sick and dying, and she was to do this with nothing but unlimited faith. The message was very clear!

When she returned to Calcutta, she told some of her community of what had happened on the train. They listened with mixed feelings and some doubt. Yet, they knew Sister Teresa was not one to have wild fantasies; she was very much down-to-earth, direct and practical.

When the archbishop of Calcutta heard of the young nun with strange ideas, he asked her to come and speak with him. Politely, firmly, fearlessly, she told him about the new work that God had called her to do, and she asked him what she should do about it.

The archbishop, convinced that the hand of God was in this, said she must leave her congregation and start a new one of her own. This was as hard for Teresa as leaving her family, for her community had been her family for the past twenty years. Here was her home, the lovely gardens, the joy of teaching young women. Now she must leave it all, for—what?

In 1948, two years after obtaining permission and approval, Sister Teresa took off the habit of the Loretto nuns and put on a simple white sari with a blue border, draped over her in the Indian style. She was now Mother Teresa of the Missionaries of Charity.

For the next three months, she studied nursing and outside dispensary work with the Medical Missionary Sisters of Patna. When she returned to Calcutta, she lived for a while with the Little Sisters of the Poor. She was comfortable with their rule of absolute poverty—no income, no bank account, no saving for a rainy day. It fit in perfectly with the life she had in mind for her new order.

But after a while, she felt she must have a place of her own. God guided her to a room in the home of a friend. Here she worked on a rule of life for her new community. The aim of the Missionaries of Charity, she wrote, "is to give wholehearted free service to the poorest of the poor, according to the teaching and life of Our Lord in the Gospel. Our particular mission is to work for their salvation and sanctification.... A Missionary of Charity must be a missionary of love. She must be full of charity in her own soul and spread that same charity to the souls of others, Christians and non-Christians."

Her first recruit arrived, a young Bengali girl who had been one of her students, and then, gradually, others came, and soon there were ten in the community. Mother Teresa first started a school for children, a school without books or chalkboard or building. She taught them the alphabet by scratching the letters into the dirt with a stick. Then she taught them hygiene, how to wash themselves and keep themselves clean.

When she found a woman dying in the street, half eaten by rats and ants, she took her to the hospital, which refused to treat her. "They take better care of their pets than their fellow man," thought Mother Teresa sadly. But she didn't let it go at that. She went to the police commissioner to complain.

He was more than happy to help her find a place where the sisters could care for these destitute dying who were an embarrassment to the government. Perhaps these holy women could relieve the pressure on him caused by people who had no place other than the streets to die.

A lovely old temple, which had been built to honor the Hindu goddess, Kali, was found vacant, and he gave it to Mother Teresa. She named it Kalighat, and it was here they brought the dying to live their last hours in sight of a loving face. She wished these frightened, lonely souls to know they were not leaving life uncared for and unloved. "They must know they too are children of God and not forgotten by him."

Next the Missionaries were guided to found a home for children—orphaned, abandoned, neglected, crippled, unwanted—and so Sishu Bhavan, the Children's Home, was started. This was followed by Shanti Nagar, the Town of Peace, a colony and rehabilitation center for lepers. At that time, two million people in India suffered from leprosy, and they were considered among the lowest caste of people in Indian society. Can you imagine how it must have been for her young Bengali nuns, who had been brought up to turn away from these "untouchables," to care for and love them?

She worked with the young nuns, training them by example as well as word. They were to treat these "least" ones as if they were Jesus, washing their bodies, treating their sores, not just a few times but every day for the rest of their lives. She encouraged the sisters to see beyond appearances and the never-ending work of giving comfort. "Make sure that you let God's grace work in your souls by accepting whatever he gives you," she said, and always, they should be joyful. "Joy is a net of love by which you can catch souls. Be kind and merciful. Let no one ever come to you without coming away better and happier...give always a happy smile."

From the beginning, Mother Teresa trusted in God alone for keeping up her homes, which were now growing and spreading all over India. Without money, she went ahead and did what those with financial sense said could not be done. Her only concern was whether the work was needed for God's glory. If so, he would send the means. "I never give money a thought," she says. "It always comes. We do all work for the Lord. He must look after us. I forget about it!"

In 1963 the archbishop blessed their companion order of the Missionary Brothers of Charity. Soon candidates were coming from other countries—England, the United Sates, Africa, Italy and other European countries—and when they were trained, they too went forth to countries that needed them and asked for their help. They minister to the poor in London, Rome, Mexico, Tanzania, Venezuela, Africa, Australia and the Philippines. In the United States they work among alcoholics, drug addicts, AIDS patients and immigrant families, as well as the sick and elderly of all races and creeds.

In Jordan and the Gaza strip, they work with Palestinian refugees, abandoned Bedouins, beggars, Christians and Muslims. The Missionaries are accepted and treated with respect by the non-Christians, for like the revered Gandhi of the Hindus, they live simply and frugally, making use of what they have, teaching self-reliance, joining prayer to work and keeping out of politics. They leave the problem of social change to others. "There are plenty of people around to do the big things," said Mother Teresa. "The Missionaries of Charity will do the little things that few are willing to do."

By 1979, her work had spread to so many countries and was so admired, she was awarded the Nobel Peace Prize. She accepted it in her usual casual manner—the glory was for God, after all, not her—and then asked that the gala dinner in her honor be canceled and the money used to feed the poor.

Today the Missionaries work in ninety countries around the world. More than three thousand men and women of every nationality have joined her orders, and millions more have formed a group called the Co-Workers of Mother Teresa, who join with her in their daily lives of prayers and sacrifices.

When she was asked near the end of her life why she, one person, decided to take on the poverty of Calcutta with all its connected problems, her answer was the same as it was some seventy years earlier:

> I was sure then and still am, that it is he and not I who
> wanted this work done. That's why I was not afraid. I knew

that if the work was mine, it would die with me. But I knew it was his work, that it will live and bring much good.
You see, I am God's pencil, a tiny bit of pencil with which he writes what he likes!

On September 5, 1997, at age eighty-seven, Mother Teresa died. On October 19, 2003, she was beatified, and the Sisters of Charity and all the world await her canonization.

ARCHBISHOP OSCAR ROMERO

Sometimes we are so wrapped up in the challenges and problems and dreams of our lives, we can't see beyond them. We know there are wars and plagues and persecutions somewhere *out there* in the world, and we may feel a momentary pang and sorrow for the people caught in them. But then we plunge back into what really concerns us—*our* world, *our* lives.

Saints and heroes see all human beings as their brothers and sisters. They take Christ's message of loving one another seriously, and that means making sure that their brothers and sisters share fully in the earthly life that is a foretaste of heaven.

This is the story of one hero and martyr who gave his life to do just that in El Salvador—Archbishop Oscar Romero. We know of other martyrs in El Salvador, including four American churchwomen and six Jesuits, their housekeeper and her daughter. Many, many more martyrs in El Salvador are known only to God and their loved ones. It is a land that has truly been "washed in the blood of martyrs," one in which acts of unbelievable cruelty and evil were committed during a twelve-year civil war.

El Salvador is the smallest republic of the Americas—"a bouillon cube of a country" it has been called. Ever since the early nineteenth century, the country has been controlled by the growers of coffee. The Spaniards first planted coffee there; other Europeans came in and joined them. Together they forced the natives, who owned the land, to give up their ownership. The natives then had no land, no homes, no one to work for except the landowners.

An American diplomat wrote in 1931, "Approximately 90% of the country's wealth is in the possession of 0.5% of the population.... They live as splendidly as kings, surrounded by crowds of servants and they send their children to be educated in Europe or the U.S. and squander money on their whims. I imagine the situation in El Salvador today is similar to France before the Revolution...."

The revolution came to El Salvador in 1931. Thirty thousand people were killed and the revolt brutally suppressed. From that time on, the nation was ruled firmly by the armed forces, while the real power still lay with the fourteen landowner families.

Oscar Romero was born into this world of grave inequality on August 15, 1917, at Ciudad Barrios, a small town which could be reached only on foot or horseback.

Oscar was a quiet, serious boy who wanted to be a priest. At the age of fourteen, he rode off to San Miguel, a seven-hour journey by horseback, to study at a preparatory seminary.

He was ordained in Rome on April 14, 1942. He returned to El Salvador and lived a traditional, conservative priestly life.

Oscar was the kind of priest who blended in well wherever he was. He rocked no boat and followed the rules, and he was well on his way to a position of prestige and power in the church. He was no threat to the rich and powerful.

In 1967 he became secretary of the Salvadoran bishops' conference. In 1970 he became auxiliary bishop of San Salvador; in 1974, bishop of Santiago de María. And on February 22, 1977, he became archbishop of San Salvador.

Many priests who were pressing for social change were disappointed in his appointment. They felt nothing would change with this man, who was the landowners' and government's choice. The new archbishop seemed to fulfill their low expectations, for he was not sympathetic to the "radical" clergy.

In one of his first interviews, Oscar stated his desire to "keep to the center, watchfully, in the traditional way." But he also said that the government "should not consider a priest who takes a stand for social justice as subversive...when he is fulfilling his mission in the pursuit of the common good." People might have thought the archbishop was merely a bland follower of rules, but he was also honest and faithful to his commitment to the gospel.

The priests in the rural districts, many of them Jesuits, were introducing ideas of social justice to the peasants. They formed small church communities in which they discussed the gospel and applied it to their own lives. They were becoming aware of the unfair oppression that had taken away their hope, and they believed that if they banded together and formed unions, the government would have to listen to them.

A few days after Oscar became archbishop, a new president took office—his name also was Romero—and he had no intention of listening or making the lives of the poor better. When fifty thousand people gathered in the Plaza Libertad in the capital to protest his election, the army troops opened fire on them, and the frightened, screaming crowd fled to the church for safety.

The archbishop could not believe what was happening. He met with his priests and spoke quietly, carefully, to them. "Go home, all of you, and take care of the people. Open your houses to any who may be in danger. Check to see if they are …being followed and, if they are, take them in and hide them." Already a transformation of his heart had begun.

Tragic events started happening, one on top of the other. Father Rutilio Grande, a Jesuit and a good friend of Oscar's, was murdered—gunned down as he rode in his Jeep with an old man and a sixteen-year-old boy. Father Grande had worked in Aguilares, a country district where the workers of the cotton and sugar cane fields lived in poverty. Father Grande had said in one of his sermons that "it is practically illegal to be an authentic Christian in our environment… where the mere proclamation of the Gospel is subversive.…"

For Oscar, it was the moment of truth, in which he looked into his soul and wondered if *he* truly proclaimed the gospel and, if so, was he prepared to take the consequences if he put Christ's message into action?

He is said to have prayed for hours by the body of his murdered friend. He had been made archbishop to stop the work of the "Marxist" priests and had believed that this was the right thing to do. But after the death of his friend, he knew he would have to choose sides. There was no middle road. Either he was with the poor or he was against them.

Oscar demanded an explanation from the government. Then he set up a committee to keep check on violations of human rights. He went to Rome to talk with Pope Paul VI to explain his actions, and the pope took Oscar's hands in his and said, "Be of good heart."

New terror had begun, increasing each day. The death-squad army groups began to burn villages, desecrate and destroy the churches, round up priests, nuns, lay ministers whom they tortured and eventually killed. Every day there were bodies lying alongside the roads; people ignored them or looked away, afraid to do anything. The army circulated handbills that read: Be a patriot, kill a priest.

The archbishop tried to walk a fine line. He condemned all violence, whether from the military or the revolutionaries (there were rebel groups apart from the church who wanted to respond as cruelly as the death squads). Yet, he made clear, the root cause for all the violence was that "the majority of men and women and above all the children...find themselves deprived of the necessities of life...and being exploited by the privileged few."

He was in trouble now with both the government and the conservative bishops who opposed any social change. Oscar's ideas of truly living the gospel were upsetting enough to make the bishops consider asking the pope to remove Oscar from office. The American and Salvadoran ambassadors to the Vatican agreed with them.

But if Oscar had enemies, he also had friends. In November 1978, he was nominated for the Nobel Peace Prize by members of the British Parliament, but the award went instead to Mother Teresa. Nonetheless, knowing that his actions had support outside his country encouraged him.

In February 1980, he went to Belgium to receive an honorary doctorate from the University of Louvain; then he went to Rome to discuss El Salvador with Pope John Paul II. When he returned to El Salvador, he wrote U.S. President Jimmy Carter, asking him not to send military aid to the government.

By now Oscar had become a serious threat to the government, and he knew he was a marked man. This did not stop him. On the First Sunday of Lent, 1980, he preached a homily on Christ's refusal to live a life of power and wealth.

Instead, Jesus had chosen "a simple life, an ordinary life....
How beautiful our country would be if we all lived this plan
of God, each one busy in his or her own job, not claiming to
dominate anyone, simply earning and eating the bread that
the family needs."

Oscar felt that his time was running out and death was near,
and he told his congregation this Sunday, March 23, as he
preached for the last time in the cathedral. "If I am killed," he
told them, "I will rise again in the people of El Salvador.... As a
pastor, I am obliged by divine decree to give my life for those I
love...even for those who may be about to kill me.... If God
accepts the sacrifice of my life, let my blood be a seed of
freedom...let my death be for the liberation of my people, as a
witness of hope in the future."

He spoke directly to the army. "Brothers, you are part of our
own people. You are killing your own brothers and sisters. No
soldier is obliged to obey an order that is contrary to the law
of God....In the name of God, and in the name of this
suffering people, whose cries rise to heaven each day...I beg
you, I plead with you, I command you in the name of God:
cease the repression!"

The government immediately condemned the archbishop's
words as "criminal" and said they amounted to treason.

The next evening, as the archbishop celebrated Mass in the
chapel of the cancer hospital where he lived, a shot rang out,
hitting and killing Oscar instantly. The lone gunman escaped.
It would be thirteen years before a special commission would
trace responsibility for the murder to a high-ranking
government official.

More than 250,000 people came to Oscar's funeral, many of
them coming by foot or bus or any means they could find. A
Protestant theologian, Doctor Jorge Lara-Braud, said these fine
words about Oscar Romero:

Together with thousands of Salvadorans, I have seen Jesus.

This time his name was Oscar Arnulfo Romero. His broken body is broken with the body of Jesus, his shed blood is shed with the blood of Jesus. And as with Jesus, so it is with Monsenor, he died for us that we might live in freedom and in love and justice for one another. His resurrection is not a future event. It is a present reality.

On May 13, 1993, the church leaders in El Salvador made the formal request for official canonization of Oscar Romero. The poor of El Salvador have no need of official approval. They know he is a saint.

THE FOUR WOMEN MARTYRS OF EL SALVADOR

After the murder of Archbishop Romero, the violence in El Salvador increased, and more U.S. missionaries responded to ease the sufferings of the people in this tormented country.

Among them were two Maryknoll nuns, Ita Ford and Maura Clarke; an Ursuline nun, Dorothy Kazel; and a lay missionary, Jean Donovan. They came from different backgrounds, were of different temperaments and ages. But their lives were woven together by the thread of compassion for the people of El Salvador.

All felt strongly drawn to this mission. They were certain it was God's will that they be there, and, even though they had no desire for death or martyrdom, they died following that will. Their lives gave witness to the radical simplicity of the gospel, and were, as Dorothy Kazel put it, "an alleluia from head to foot."

Dorothy Kazel

Dorothy Kazel was born on June 30, 1939, in Cleveland, Ohio, to Lithuanian-American parents, Joseph and Malvina Kazel. She was cheerful and fun-loving and extremely pretty, and her family was close-knit and happy.

After graduating from college in 1960, she joined the Ursuline order of nuns and began teaching at Sacred Heart Academy in East Cleveland, an inner-city school. She worked there for seven years. Her friends of those days remember a young woman of high energy and fun, never afraid to be first—first to hop on a motorcycle, first to play a practical joke and first to accept a challenge.

In the late 1960s she learned that the Cleveland diocese was forming a mission to go to El Salvador. Dorothy volunteered but wasn't chosen. She tried again six years later and this time she was chosen. She and another nun, Sister Martha Owen, left Cleveland in the summer of 1974, heading for language school in Costa Rica to learn Spanish.

They began work in the village of La Libertad, El Salvador, where they filled the religious needs of the community and traveled around setting up libraries and hygiene classes and distributing food and medicines.

They also tried to give the people a sense of their own worth, reminding them that they were children of God, deserving of basic human rights, and that they had the power to change the injustices in their lives. It was because of this encouragement that the ruling class and the army labeled the nuns "subversive."

The spiritual side of Dorothy's breezy nature blossomed in El Salvador. She read the Scriptures daily, finding the Holy Spirit's guidance in them. She gave up little pleasures and comforts as a sacrifice for those she knew were suffering in her adopted country.

After five years in El Salvador, Martha returned to Cleveland

and Dorothy stayed behind to train her replacement, a young woman who had recently joined the team. Her name was Jean Donovan.

Jean Donovan

Jean was born April 10, 1953, to Raymond and Patricia Donovan, an Irish-American couple. She and her older brother, Michael, lived a comfortable, middle-class life with their parents in Westport, Connecticut.

Like Dorothy, Jean was outgoing, adventurous and ready to take on a challenge. She was also strong-willed, with a tendency to take over, a trait which rubbed even her friends the wrong way. But this was balanced by a deep concern for others, and she would not intentionally hurt anyone's feelings. She just wanted to do things *her* way.

In 1971, like other students who could afford it, Jean spent her junior year in college abroad as an exchange student. At University College Cork in Ireland, she met the person who would guide her into her future work, Father Michael Crowley, the college chaplain.

Every Monday evening, about forty students gathered at his campus home to discuss world problems, especially Latin American poverty, since Father Crowley had recently returned from working in Peru. He advised the students that when they graduated and got "a nice job, don't become a nice comfy capitalist. Feel it as your Christian duty to change the wrong structures around you...."

The seed had been planted, but it lay dormant while Jean finished college and took a job in the Cleveland branch of a large accounting firm. Now with an impressive salary to indulge in, Jean and her cousin, Colleen, rented an apartment in an exclusive area. She bought a new car and motorcycle and enjoyed her new lifestyle immensely.

Now and then Father Crowley's words came back to haunt her: "...don't become a nice comfy capitalist...." Eventually the little seed began to sprout. After much soul-searching, she wondered if she had the makings of a missionary. To find out, she began working with inner-city children in a diocesan program and then made plans to go to El Salvador.

At a farewell party, one of her friends teased her, "What are you going to El Salvador for anyway, Jean? So you can be known as Saint Jean the Playful?" She replied, "Look, it's a can't-lose situation for me. Either I will get three years of great experience out of it or I will die—and then you'll have to pray to Saint Jean the Playful for the rest of your life!"

She left for Maryknoll for her missionary training in the fall of 1978, then studied in language school in Guatemala before leaving for La Libertad, where Dorothy Kazel awaited her. She and Dorothy became fast friends—they were kindred spirits in having fun and spreading it around.

A friend of Dorothy's wrote: "Jean and Dorothy lived under rather primitive conditions—no hot water, no indoor plumbing.... Their main source of entertainment...were the antics of their three cats whose job it was to keep the cockroach and lizard population under control....Despite all the dangers they faced daily, they considered themselves very ordinary."

Jean was a great admirer of Oscar Romero. "It is so inspiring when you see and hear a man like Archbishop Romero," she said. "He really is the voice of the people. The way they respond to him...is like the Pope when enters church. They stand on the pews and clap for him."

She had been in El Salvador for only eight months when Romero was assassinated. Jean had come to La Libertad with very conservative views and spoke scornfully of the revolutionaries. But the unfair poverty, the killing of the catechists and death of the archbishop all combined to change her belief in the rightness of the government. Now she agreed with the archbishop's request to President Jimmy Carter not to send aid to the government.

In spite of the increasing danger, she could not bear to think of leaving "her" people. In a letter to a friend she wrote, "Now I must assess my own position because I am not up for suicide. Several times I have decided to leave—I almost could except for the children, the poor bruised victims of adult lunacy. Who would care for them? Whose heart would be so staunch as to favor the reasonable thing in a sea of their tears and loneliness? Not mine...."

Ita Ford

Ita Ford was born April 23, 1940, in Bay Ridge, Brooklyn, the second of three children of Mildred and William Ford. She was a small, slight child, "with sparkling eyes and elfin grin" that lit up her face, an expression she kept all her life.

When she was in high school, she began thinking of joining the Maryknoll Sisters. The Maryknollers were well-known to her, because her uncle, Francis X. Ford, was a Maryknoll bishop who had died in a Chinese prison when she was twelve. So in September 1961, she entered the Maryknoll Sisters' motherhouse in Ossining, New York, and at once she knew she was home.

In a letter home Ita wrote, "It's wonderful to be called. It's dizzying to know you're loved.... It's a little like the 'Hound of Heaven'—you run smack into God." Before she made her first vows, however, she became quite sick, and the Mother General felt Ita should not make them. She offered up her disappointment, pulled herself together and got a job as editor in a religious publishing house.

She became involved in protests against the Vietnam War and demonstrations for civil rights. She taught catechism to Puerto Rican students, and she read to the blind. Still, she could not dislodge her strong yearning to be a Maryknoller. She decided to try again, and this time she was accepted.

By March 1973, she was on her way to her first assignment in Chile, where she worked for five years. When she returned home for the Maryknollers' year of reflection, she read about the tragic situation in El Salvador. She wanted this to be her next assignment, and so it was. In April 1980 Ita and her good friend, Sister Carla Piette, came to the mission at Chalatenango, in the northern province of El Salvador.

Ita and Carla worked beautifully as a team. They went everywhere together on their rounds of transporting refugees and providing them with food and medicine and shelter. But after only three months together, Carla lost her life in a freak accident.

They were driving across a swollen river, when the torrents swept up the Jeep and threw it on its side. Before she drowned, Carla pushed Ita through the window, and she was swept downstream. Ita resigned herself to dying, but a voice said within her, "The Lord has saved you to continue serving the poor...." Suddenly she saw tree roots and pulled herself up onto the bank.

Despite her sorrow at Carla's death, Ita insisted on remaining at Chalatenango. Another Maryknoll nun, Maura Clarke, had volunteered to take Carla's place.

Maura Clarke

Maura Clarke was born in New York City on January 13, 1931, the oldest of the three children of John and Mary McCloskey Clarke.

During her freshman year at college, Maura, like Ita, felt called to become a Maryknoll nun, so in September 1950, she left college and entered Maryknoll. In 1954 she received her bachelor's degree in education.

She had hoped and prayed to be assigned to an African mission, but instead she was sent to the Bronx, where she learned firsthand about the violent life of the poor, "hearing the children's stories about their mothers being beaten, fathers slashed, brothers shot...."

After five years in the Bronx, Maura was sent to Nicaragua, where she was principal of the school and superior of the community. Besides teaching the children, the nuns helped the people form small Christian communities and work toward better conditions in their lives.

When Maura returned to the United States in 1976, she worked for three years and then felt the tug to go back to "the people I love," so she responded to a plea from Maryknoll for volunteers to work in El Salvador. When she got there, Maura was shocked to find that the violence was much worse than in Nicaragua. She wrote to her parents about the town being filled with squads of military police, watching the nuns in the hope they would be caught in some "subversive" activity. "The way innocent people...are cut up with machetes and blessed temples of the Lord thrown and left for buzzards...seems unbelievable but it happens every day....Being here with Ita and working for the refugees has its sweetness, consolation, special grace....At times one wonders if one should remain in such a crazy incredible mess. I only know that I am trying to follow where the Lord leads, and in spite of fear and uncertainty at times, I feel at peace and joyful...."

December 2, 1980

In late November 1980 Ita and Maura attended the annual assembly of Maryknoll Sisters in Nicaragua. They closed the meeting on the evening of December 1 and left by plane the next day for El Salvador. They would be picked up by their friends from La Libertad, Dorothy and Jean.

On Thanksgiving Day, Jean and Dorothy had met the ambassador from the United States, Robert White and his wife, MaryAnn, at an ecumenical service. The ambassador invited them to dinner on the night of December 1, and they happily accepted.

They stayed overnight at the ambassador's home and left in a white van the next morning after breakfast, planning to do some shopping before picking up their friends at the airport.

When Jean and Dorothy arrived at the airport, they found that Ita and Maura had been delayed and would not come in until 6 P.M. They returned and all four friends rejoiced in being reunited and set off for La Libertad, eager to get back and have a homecoming party.

When the four women did not return that night or the next morning, the priest at the mission became concerned. None of the nuns had kept appointments, none were where they should have been, and no one had seen them.

On the afternoon of December 3, their white van was found on the road to La Libertad. It had been burned and blackened by fire inside and out and stripped of license plates, tools or anything that could identify it.

One the morning of December 4, a farmer called the village priest and told him that there were bodies of four foreign women in a shallow grave by the side of a dirt road. They were wearing sandals, and very few Salvadoran women could afford sandals.

The priest notified the archbishop who called the American ambassador. By noon, the ambassador and the American consul confirmed that these were the bodies of the missionaries.

They had been shot, beaten, tortured. When, after years of investigation, it was determined that six officers of the national guard had done the deed, the reason they gave for murdering the women was that they were "subversive."

Maura and Ita were buried in a country cemetery in Chalatenango, according to Maryknoll custom. A funeral Mass was held in La Libertad for Dorothy and Jean before their bodies were returned to the United States. As dawn broke across the night sky, the caskets passed through the crowd, from shoulder to shoulder, and triumphant applause spread from the church to the people waiting outside in the square, and along the route leading to the airport, continuing as the plane lifted off from the land they had loved and died in.

The night before the murder, at the closing liturgy of the assembly in Nicaragua, Ita read a passage from one of Archbishop Romero's homilies:

> Christ invites us not to fear persecution because...the one who is committed to the poor must share the same fate as the poor. And in El Salvador we know what the fate of the poor signifies: to disappear, to be tortured, to be held captive, and to be found dead by the side of the road.

By traveling that road, the road to martyrdom, Dorothy, Jean, Ita and Maura had indeed become alleluias "from head to foot"!

GIANNA MOLLA

Some saints were so anxious to get back to heaven, they turned their backs on this world and wanted nothing to do with it. They would not stop to smell the flowers or enjoy a feast or play with a child, for they believed nothing on earth could possibly compare with what awaited them in heaven. They went into monasteries or became hermits in the forest or desert, so they wouldn't be tempted by earthly delights.

We can admire and respect them, but we don't often find them as lovable as those holy humans who have given themselves to God but still live in and enjoy this world. Such a person was Gianna Molla.

She was born in Magenta, Italy, in 1922, on the feast day of Saint Francis of Assisi, October 4, the tenth child of Alberto and Maria Beretta. They were strict, loving, deeply religious parents dedicated to raising "a garden of saints," and, since they were Third Order Franciscans, instilling in them a Franciscan spirit of joy and simplicity.

There were thirteen children in all, raised in a home centered in Christ and the sacraments. Everything they did—studying, serving the needy, going to concerts and vacationing in the Alps, taking care of each other—revolved around their duty and their gratitude to God. Gifts had been given to be shared and used as blessings for others and to give honor to God. This was why they were here.

The Beretta family seemed too good to be true. How could life in a family of thirteen strong-willed, independent children be the haven of lighthearted peace it was? Can you imagine the noise at mealtimes? Alberto and Maria did not leave behind a manual of instructions for the perfect family; they simply loved God well and taught their children to do the same. Maria encouraged her children to "always in whatever state you are called, be faithful to the Sacred Heart...Our Lady, Saint Joseph and Saint Francis...."

In her will, Maria asked her children to "love their father very much and not to let him be alone. Try to live together in the family as long as possible. If the Lord calls you to serve him, go to him, but whoever remains at home should keep Father company."

It was this kind of family in which Gianna grew up. Even on the outside, she reflected serenity, and she had a dark, quiet beauty about her. Her black eyes had "a deep, tender look, she caressed with her look," and, always, she was smiling. She had absorbed her parents' ability to enjoy beauty in all its forms—in music and art, in trees and children and, especially, the mountains.

She loved skiing and mountain climbing. A photo shows her with a rope tied around her waist and an ice-axe in her hand as she climbed to the summit of Mount Rosa in the Alps. "It is so wonderful," she said, "when we are high up, with a clear sky and white snow, how we enjoy and praise the Lord. I feel so happy...I would spend hours contemplating it!"

In 1942, when she was twenty, Gianna entered the University of Milan to study medicine. She believed it was God's will that she become a doctor. It was her way to serve and, as she said, firmly "live the Will of God every moment and live it with joy."

Gianna received her degree in medicine and surgery in November 1949, and immediately began practicing in the town of Mesero, about five miles from her parents' home in Magenta, where she still lived. To get to Mesero, she traveled the narrow, winding dirt road on her bike or motorcycle. At the same time, she continued her studies for a degree in pediatrics (medical care for children), which she received in July 1952.

To be a doctor was both mission and vocation for Gianna. In healing her clients' bodies, she would also help heal their souls. It was almost like being a priest, she said "for we have occasions that a priest does not have. Our mission does not end when medicines are of no use any longer. There is the soul to be led to God and your word would have the authority.... The priest can touch Jesus...so we touch Jesus in the bodies of our patients."

She believed that although body and soul were different, "they are united.... God...has grafted the divine in the human so that whatever we do has greater value."

Gianna was happy in her work but felt the need to do more. She thought of joining her brother, Alberto, a doctor and a priest, as a lay missionary in Brazil. She was ready to leave but obstacles kept popping up, one after the other. She wrote to Alberto, "Everybody is giving me contrary advice...they are dissuading me because, as a woman, I may not be able to stand the climate."

Alberto responded that perhaps they were right. Perhaps she should consider marriage as her "missionary work." He advised her to think about it. But Gianna was determined.

She was going to Brazil, and that was that.

Then one day an engineer named Pietro Molla came into the clinic to visit another doctor. Gianna and Pietro were introduced, looked into each other's eyes, murmured polite how-do-you-dos and went about their business, knowing something important had happened. Everywhere they went, they would bump into each other—at stores, Catholic Action meetings, on the road—and each time, they smiled and talked a little longer.

Gianna began to change her mind about marriage. In 1954 she went as accompanying doctor for the sick on a pilgrimage to Lourdes, France. She told a friend, "I asked our Lady what I should do—go to the missions or marry? When I reached home...Pietro came in!" She had her answer.

And so on September 24, 1955, Gianna and Pietro were married. They were happy and eager to begin this new chapter in their lives. They had found a home at Ponte Nuova, a short distance from Magenta. In a letter to Pietro, Gianna wrote, "While we were choosing our furniture, I had a foretaste of a little, beautiful, shining new house....Pietro, just think of our nest, warmed by our love and rendered happy by the beautiful children God will send us....Let us raise our hearts high and live happily!" That she did, for the rest of her brief, full life.

After their marriage, Gianna continued her work at the clinic, even though Pietro had suggested she give it up. She knew she was needed. In the morning she visited her patients in their homes; in the afternoon she held office hours in the clinic. Often she was more than a doctor; she found work for fathers desperate to keep their families together, and she charged the sick who were poor nothing and gave them free medicine and money.

When she was working, her patients called her "the mother in the white overalls," but when she was at home or out with her husband, Gianna loved to look like the lady she was. She read fashion magazines from Paris and circled the dresses she thought right for her. She wore simple, elegant clothes and red nail polish and had her hair done, for she felt that "to present herself elegantly is self-respect, it is a sign of love for others, it is the glorification of Him who created beauty."

Her husband, who had a habit of writing letters to her even when he wasn't traveling, wrote, "You have shown me that we can do the will of God fully and become saints without renouncing the fullness of the pure and best joys that life and creation can offer us."

In 1956 the first of their "beautiful children," Pierluigi, arrived, followed by Maria Zita (Mariolina) in 1957 and Laura (Lauretta) in 1959.

In the summer of 1961 Gianna was delighted to know another baby was on the way, but along with this happy news, there was disturbing news as well. A large tumor had been found attached to her womb. There would have to be an operation to remove it and, she was advised, the baby as well.

To try to save the baby would be risky for both mother and child. But Gianna was determined that this baby be given a chance to live. "If you have to choose between me and the child, do not hesitate...first, the life of the child. I demand it. Save the child!"

The tumor was removed and the baby left untouched. Even though the operation was successful, there would be the danger of Gianna's losing the baby at any time during the next six months. Gianna and Pietro and all their friends and family prayed that this would not be so. They asked for the miracle of a healthy baby.

On April 21, Good Friday, Gianna entered the hospital. She told a friends, "I am not sure of coming back...they will have to save one of us and I want that my child should live." The tumor and the difficult pregnancy had left her with many concerns about her health. Before she left her home, Gianna made sure the children's clothes were washed and pressed, the refrigerator and cupboards full. If she was not coming back, she wanted to be sure her family was taken care of.

The next day, Holy Saturday, a daughter was born, as healthy and pink and chubby as her parents had prayed. But before Gianna's delivery, a fatal infection (peritonitis) had set in. For almost a week, Gianna suffered with the pain and fever, and on April 28, 1962, she died.

A day later, her daughter was baptized: Gianna Emanuela.

In a letter Pietro wrote to Gianna after her death, he said, "You did not do exceptional things...you did not seek heroism. You were aware of and did your duty as a young woman, as a wife, as a mother and doctor with full availability to the plans and will of God....Already on that morning of tears...we were sure you were in heaven...whoever is in heaven is a saint, and I...am sure of your sanctity."

So were others. In 1978 the pope received a letter from the archbishops and bishops of Lombardy urging that her name be submitted for beautification, for "Gianna Molla has fulfilled in her brief life of 40 years, the commandment of love ... that consists in giving one's life for those we love and becomes a courageous example of Christian behavior."

On April 24, 1994, Gianna Molla was beautified by Pope John Paul II. Among those celebrating this joyful event were her husband, Pietro, and her family, which includes a young physician, Dr. Gianna Emanuela Molla, the daughter whom Gianna chose to save.

DOCTOR THOMAS DOOLEY

Sometimes we imagine saints and heroes as people set apart
from us. We can't see them eye to eye because we have to look
up to them. We see them as noble, intense, unwavering in
their zeal to be holy, unflinching in their resolve not to sin. It's
a little overwhelming. There they are, up on their pedestals,
sacrificing and doing penance, while we lie draped over a
couch or in a hammock, eating a Milky Way, reading about
them but not connecting with them.

So every now and then, it's very satisfying to come across a
hero whose humanity we can recognize and enjoy, someone
like Doctor Thomas Dooley, who liked to drive fast in a red
convertible, dance the jitterbug, go to parties and play
practical jokes. (He gave his brother a wooden cigar store
Indian as a wedding present.)

Thomas Anthony Dooley was born on January 17, 1927, in St. Louis, Missouri. He led a comfortable, upper-middle-class life with his parents, two younger brothers and an older stepbrother. Tom, says his mother, was always a leader, confident and strong-willed. He would never refuse a dare. He had a gift for music (he played the piano) and languages, especially French.

It would seem that his gifts were leading him to an artistic career, but Tom wanted nothing else but to be a doctor. His father did not agree with his decision; he felt Tom had too much impatience and quick temper to persevere in medical school. Nonetheless, Tom's mind was made up. At the age of sixteen he entered the University of Notre Dame in a premed course.

For awhile, it seemed his father might have been right. Tom had an active social life, going to dances, concerts, parties and football games. He planned to become a society doctor and specialize in obstetrics (delivering babies). The Tom Dooley of college days gave no hint of the Doctor Dooley who would one day devote his life to healing the sick and needy of Vietnam and Laos. He probably had not even heard of those countries then.

In 1944, during World War II, he left Notre Dame to enlist as a Navy medical corpsman. One reason for his decision was that his beloved stepbrother, Earle, was already fighting in Europe. Tom spent the next two years at the Great Lakes Naval Training Station. After the war was over, he returned to Notre Dame to finish his medical studies.

These were years of spiritual growth for Tom. He often went to the Grotto devoted to Mary on the Notre Dame campus to think and pray and wonder about his life. Under his brash energy and frivolity, his compassionate and sensitive soul was being urged to be more and do more. In a letter written to Father Theodore Hesburgh, then president of the university, near the end of his life, Tom spoke lovingly about the Grotto:

> Notre Dame is…on my mind and always in my heart. That
> Grotto is the rock to which my life is anchored…away from
> the Grotto, Dooley just prays.…There must be snow
> everywhere and the lake is ice glass. . . and the priests are
> bundled in their too-large, too long old black coats.…If I
> could go to the Grotto now, then I think I could sing inside.
> I could be full of faith and poetry and loveliness and know
> more beauty, tenderness and compassion.…

After graduation from Notre Dame in 1948, he entered St.
Louis University Medical School and received his doctor of
medicine degree in 1953. He returned to the Navy as an officer
in the Medical Corps, determined not to be just a good doctor
but the *best* doctor in the fleet.

Tom was stationed overseas at an air force base in Guam,
and then to the Naval Air Station in Yokosuka, Japan. He was
excited about living in Japan, for he had a great interest in
Asian culture and the Buddhist religion. He was entranced by
everything Asian, and as soon as possible learned to speak
Japanese.

"If we could only learn more about these people," he said,
"if we could present our ways, our government, our
convictions about freedom to them more successfully.…We in
America have so much, yet we are gradually becoming hated
by the Eastern world because of our actions abroad.…We
must make our American dreams Asian realities."

He had his chance to put his words into action when his ship
received orders to take part in the evacuation of North
Vietnam. There had been a civil war going on in the country
before the United States became involved in the conflict. A
treaty signed in Geneva divided Vietnam in half: The northern
part went to the communists; the southern part was to be a free
republic. Anyone wishing to relocate from north to south could
do so up to May 1955, leaving from the city of Haiphong.

Tom's ship arrived in Haiphong filled with canned food, medical supplies, blankets and other necessities, ready to bring the refugees to freedom in the south. For the next eleven months, his ship and others carried these refugees, who were in poor health, to the port of Saigon. In Haiphong, a medical processing camp was set up because the refugees poured in at such a rate that the ships could not keep up with them, and the refugees had to be put somewhere.

Since many diseases were brought in with refugees, Tom started a DDT decontamination station and disease-screening examinations so the preventive medicine team could learn everything possible about the sickness of the area, such as dysentery, hepatitis and trachoma, an eye disease.

The people were losing their fear of Americans and began calling Tom "Bac Sy My," which means "Good American Doctor." He was deeply moved by their gratitude. "No one ever seems to have treated their eyes," he said. "No one ever set up living improvements for them, no one ever chlorinated water....The Viets always thought of America as an extension of France" (which had taken over Vietnam as a colony). "Now the people are seeing Americans for themselves, and they find that we are gentle people, and a people who want to aid them...."

By October 1954, over 350,000 people had been evacuated by air and sea lift. For the rescuers, it was not always a happy, pleasant experience. "Many of the sailors were angered with the refugees. They smell bad, have awful-looking diseases, don't understand English....I tried to show the boys that they are really a fine and noble people, that they are undergoing tribulations that many of us Americans could never endure.... They are cold, wet and sick....They have heard rumors that they will be gassed and tortured by Americans....These people are not a stinking mass of humanity, but a great people, distressed."

Tom wrote to his mother and his friends at Notre Dame, asking for help for "my children," and they sent socks and underwear and toys and treats. He wrote to drug and vitamin and soap companies requesting samples of their products and soon the responses began pouring into the medical station. Tom's work of helping people to people, heart to heart, had begun.

On May 12, 1955, the North Vietnamese arrived to take over Haiphong. Tom and the American officers were flown out of the city on the last American plane out—with one extra passenger: a five-foot statue of Our Lady of Fatima, which Tom had saved from the altar of the church at Haiphong. Tom had hated the thought of its being desecrated by the incoming communists, so he requested permission of the priest to bring it with him, and the priest agreed. "I took an American aid blanket, we lowered the statue from the altar, I stole it out to the airport, put it on the plane and brought it to Saigon. They were jubilant!"

He then left Saigon for his home base in Japan, where he began work on his first book, *Deliver Us From Evil*, which told the story of the last days of Haiphong. He decided to apply for a residency in orthopedics at the national Naval Medical Center in Bethesda, Maryland. When he arrived in California, instead of flying from there to his home in St. Louis, he decided to take a train because he wanted to see again "America's fields and mountains, her canyons and plains.... I was back in America, though truly I had never left her at all. She was in my heart."

He went on to New York City to meet with a publisher interested in his book, and then set out to give the lectures across the country telling of the plight of the Vietnamese people and their urgent needs, and also explaining the history of this faraway, little-known region.

He told what he and his handful of helpers had accomplished.

"We had seen simple, tender, loving care…change a people's fear and hatred into friendship.…It made me proud to be a doctor…who had…witnessed the enormous possibilities of medical aid in all its Christlike power and simplicity."

Then, to his family and friends' surprise, he reversed his decision about further study. He told his mother, "I'm resigning from the navy, and I'm going to Laos" (a small neighboring country of Vietnam). He had the dream of creating a medical program, which he would finance by his writing, lecturing and begging. He would not be sponsored by any government or religion.

Part of the plan was to live with the people, "learning the characteristics of their honest and gentle Buddhist life. We have no intention of trying to foist our way of life on them, nor convert them. The only aim is 50% medicine and 50% contact with Americans who simply want to help."

He brought his ideas to the Cambodian and Laotian diplomats in Washington, and they were very interested, but puzzled. "Doctor Dooley," asked one, "why should you, a young man with a career before you, choose to make this sacrifice?"

In answer, Tom quoted one of his medical corpsmen, "We just want to do what we can for people who ain't got it so good!" There were no more questions and permission was granted.

On August 7, 1956, Tom and three coworkers left San Francisco, bound for the village of Van Vieng in Laos. Awaiting them there was a small dilapidated house on stilts, under which the neighborhood pigs, cows and chickens foraged for food, and another small building which would be their hospital. From the very first day, patients lined up for treatment. Besides infections and injuries, they suffered from beriberi, malaria and tuberculosis.

Tom was happy in his work. He called himself "a jungle doctor, practicing nineteenth-century medicine. All of us here are out of contact with what is usually termed civilization: plumbing, hot water, television...but we are learning...that there is an intense joy that comes from serving others."

When he saw the children he had healed smile, he wrote, "At such moments I remembered just why we were here. Maybe the dream of Anne Frank" (the young Jewish girl who died in a German concentration camp) "is closer than we know: 'Things will change and men will become good again and these pitiless days will come to an end and the world will once more know order, rest, peace.'"

The clinic was such a success, Tom was asked by the prime minister of Laos if he would move the unit to the northern tip of the country to the mountain village of Nam Tha to work with the people there, and he agreed.

Sadly Tom and his coworkers left their friends in Van Vieng, who tied cotton strings of friendship on the wrists of the four Americans, chanting:

> May you possess all wisdom and health,
> May you have many wives,
> May your airplane not fall from the sky,
> May you always carry our love with you,
> May you return to us, your friends.

In Nam Tha, they set up a clinic and a hospital and went to work treating the tribal mountain people with as much compassion and care as they had the people of Van Vieng. In September 1958, Tom decided to return to the United States to try to put his plan for medical mission into action. He would call the program Medico. Teams of volunteer doctors and nurses would work not only in Asia but around the world, and would be financed by public donations. On his way home, he stopped off at Lambarene, Africa, to visit Doctor Albert Schweitzer, one of Tom's heroes and inspirations. Doctor

Schweitzer said he would help in any way he could. "I do not know what your destiny will be," he told Tom, "but this I know. You will always have happiness if you seek and find how to serve."

Now Tom had three jobs going at once—his work in Laos, setting up Medico and raising funds for it, and work on his second book, *The Edge of Tomorrow*. By September 1958, he was ready to return to Laos. His lecture tour had brought in gifts of medicines, equipment and $300,000 in cash gifts. He returned to Laos, to the village of Muong Sing, elated and eager to get back to work.

Medico programs spread from Laos and Cambodia to Hong Kong and Jordan and Africa, with more and more requests coming in from other countries asking for help. Then, in the midst of all his work, Tom discovered a small lump in his chest which turned out to be malignant. He was ordered to return to the United States immediately for surgery.

The operation removed all the cancer, he was told, and the future looked bright. He rejoiced that "the jagged, ugly cancer scar went no deeper than my flesh.... There was no cancer of my spirit.... Whatever time was left...I would continue to help the clots and clusters of withered and wretched in Asia to the utmost of my ability.... Now...I was a member of the fellowship of those who bear the mark of pain."

He returned to Laos and resumed his work, but the cancer reappeared. By Christmas, 1960, his condition had so worsened that on Christmas night, he left by plane for a New York hospital, leaving forever that world he loved so much.

On the evening of January 18, 1961, Tom Dooley, barely thirty-four years old, died. Six months later his family and friends began the Thomas A. Dooley Foundation, which carried on his dreams of developing medical care systems, health education, disease prevention and medical aid to refugees. In 1980 its name was changed to The Dooley

Foundation/Intermed, and its intent and purpose then was to help the needy sick of El Salvador, Nicaragua, Honduras, Haiti and other Third World countries.

Tom was not a meek and humble hero. He attracted criticism like flypaper draws flies. He has been called "tyrannical and egotistical," and his temper was as quick as his wit. But he said his critics didn't bother him. "I am a doctor— in my valley I have some forty thousand human beings.... Without me they have smallpox, diphtheria, typhoid, cholera....My satisfaction comes from what I do, not from what someone may say about me...that's what really counts.... Besides, a man who lifts his head above the crowd is bound to get hit with rotten fruit."

But with children, he was never or brusque or impatient. His message for teenagers who wrote him for advice was this:

> You are going to be the ones to grow up and fulfill destiny ...please prepare yourselves now for what you must do in the future. Education can be a time bomb. You are assembled now in the classroom, but the explosion comes at a later date....Learn the things you must learn. Reach out beyond the campus and beyond the continent that you live in....Understand that there is one rule above all other rules, the moral law of God. Work hard in school, amass the things and facts you must need now, and later in your life, when the challenge is flung at you, stand up high, and tall and strong, and answer it...and answer it well.

MYCHAL JUDGE

Of all the heroes in this book, Father Mychal Judge may be the one you already know. You've seen his picture in the newspapers and on television, as the priest who died while anointing a fallen firefighter at the World Trade Center tragedy on September 11, 2001.

But he was not only a recognizable man of our time; he was a man who could be one of us. He could have been a big brother, a godfather, a coach, a favorite uncle who took you to ball games and let you eat too many hot dogs. He could have come to dinner as part of the family.

But if he had not been the first registered casualty of the tragedy, we might never have known of him. Only those in his immediate circle—the population of New York City—knew him as the unique reflection of God that he was. Now, we all know him as one who lay down his life for his friends, and that makes him a hero, and, in Catholic eyes, a martyr. He died for the joy of serving God and his "boys," the firefighters.

Robert Emmet Judge was born on May 11, 1933, in Brooklyn, the son of Irish immigrants who ran a boardinghouse. When he was six years old, his father died, and Robert tried to fill his shoes in taking care of his mother and his sisters, Erin, and Dymphna, his twin. He became the handyman of the family, fixing and patching things up and running errands. He often went into Manhattan and set up shoe-shining stands in Grand Central and Penn stations to earn money to help at home.

While he was there, he often stopped in at St. Francis of Assisi Church, which was near Penn Station. He loved the oasis of peace in the noisy city, the smell of incense, the lower church and the fountain. He had a favorite friar. "I loved him and his brown robe. I used to follow him around everywhere," he said. "I knew even then I wanted to be a friar."

At the age of fifteen, he entered the Franciscan St. Joseph's Seraphic Seminary in Callicoon, New York. He professed his final vows in 1958 and was ordained in 1961, taking the name of Michael (he only changed the spelling to Mychal much later to lessen the confusion, because there were so many Michaels living at the rectory). He spent two years as assistant to the president of Siena College in Loudonville, New York, and the next twenty-three as pastor of two churches in New Jersey, and then traveled to England for a year at the Franciscan house of studies in Canterbury.

When he came back, in 1986, he was assigned to be pastor at the church of St. Francis in New York City, the very one that welcomed him after a day of shining shoes. How that must have delighted his Irish heart, which saw God's hand in every coincidence!

A few days after his arrival, he answered a hospital call to celebrate Mass for a policeman, Steven McDonald, who had been shot on duty and was paralyzed. That night began a friendship, not only with Steven but also his wife and son, that lasted until Mychal's death. Together they traveled to Lourdes and several times to Ireland to encourage reconciliation between the Catholics and Protestants in a country wearied by war.

In 1992, Mychal was appointed chaplain of the New York Fire Department. He was elated. He said if he hadn't become a priest, he would have been a firefighter. Now he had the best of both worlds.

Being a priest and firefighting was a natural match for Mychal. "Priests and firefighters both enter people's lives at a point of crisis," he said, "and they have similar outlooks on life—it's the need to help, to rescue."

He won the hearts of the firefighters simply by being himself. He loved being with people, telling jokes, singing old Irish songs and making people laugh. And like Solanus Casey, he knew how to listen and give his complete attention to whatever need was present. He became part of the firefighters' families, and officiated at baptisms, weddings, funerals, made hospital visits and remembered every birthday with cards and gifts.

He was even more a source of comfort to them in dark times—deaths on the job, family trials, money problems, sickness and addictions. He was a member of Alcoholics Anonymous and called their twelve-step program "America's greatest contribution to spirituality." He gave encouragement to those recovering from addiction because he was one of them.

When Mychal wasn't on call with the firefighters (sometimes nineteen hours a day), he was everywhere and anywhere. "He was the busiest man alive," said one of the firefighters. He worked on bread lines, soup kitchens, with the homeless and with AIDS patients. A true New Yorker, born and raised there, earthy, streetwise, he embraced and basked in the life of it, the noise, traffic, chaos, smells and characters. And yet his priorities were not worldly. He had no use for "things." Gifts given to him found their way to the homeless. His room at the friary was spare and uncluttered. Once he said to a fellow friar, "You know what I need? Absolutely nothing! I don't need a thing in the world. I am the happiest man on the face of the earth."

He walked everywhere, briskly. He walked the Brooklyn Bridge at least once a week, got an ice-cream cone at Brighton Beach, then turned around and walked back home. "I love to look at the Statue of Liberty," he said, "the lights of the city, the Verrazano Bridge, the Manhattan Bridge carrying the subway cars. The city is just the most extraordinary place to live!" And he never left the friary without a wad of dollar bills to give to the homeless.

When the day's work was done, Mychal spent the evening hours, usually past midnight, writing letters and making phone calls, making the final call to his firehouse, Engine 1, Ladder 24, which he could see from his window. As soon as a firefighter picked up, Mychal would wave goodnight to him. And when he woke around 6:30 A.M., the first thing he did was get down on his knees and give thanks for another day of sobriety and pray his prayer:

> Lord, take me where you want me to go,
> Let me meet who you want me to meet,
> Tell me what you want me to say
> And keep me out of Your way.

His spirituality was simple, direct and honest. When he became a priest, he said, "I had no idea what life I'd have…you just take one day at a time. I don't get into tomorrow because God hasn't created it yet. So I live in today as best I can for the glory of God and His people." And how he loved his people! He blessed everyone, whether they wanted it or not. "He was absolutely hands-on," said a friend. "Religion didn't make any difference for him—he was the same towards everyone, regardless of their beliefs."

He believed God gave him a special grace to face stressful

situations. "There is no question about it....I, Mychal Judge, am not capable of doing these things on my own." He prayed to Maximilian Kolbe every day. "His story is absolutely extraordinary. It is definitely God's grace. The wonderful thing about that is saying 'yes' and accepting that grace....It takes courage in the midst of fear and you do it with the grace of God."

On the morning of September 10, 2001, Mychal spoke at the dedication of a renovated firehouse. He told the firefighters:

> We come to this house this morning to celebrate renewal, new life....We can never thank God enough for the reality of the lives we have....You do what God has called you to do. You show up, you put one foot in front of another, you get on that rig, you go out to do the job, which is a mystery and a surprise. You have no idea when you get on that rig, no matter how big the call, no matter how small, you have no idea what God's calling you to, but He needs you...."

The next day the call that came would be big. It was a glorious September morning with the bluest sky filled with puffs of white clouds—the kind of day you thank God for. Before noon, the two towers of the World Trade Center had collapsed, killing almost three thousand people, over three hundred and fifty of them firefighters. Mychal sped to the scene, getting there in time to bless a bunch of firefighters running into Tower Number One. When they looked back, they saw him running to minister to someone on the ground. He took off his helmet and was giving last rites to a fallen firefighter when a shower of debris suddenly fell on Mychal's head and he was killed.

When the firefighters found him, they carried him to a nearby church, St. Peter's on Barclay Street, and laid him on the altar, his helmet and badge placed in tribute on his chest. "In a world that was gray and dark...lying on the altar was the body of Mychal Judge," said one. "In a horrendous moment, it was a beautiful sight." Later that day, they brought him back to his firehouse, Engine 1, Ladder 24, and laid him on a cot. They formed a circle around him, got down on their knees and started to cry, grieving for Father Mike, their friend.

On the day of his funeral, Father Michael Duffy, a Franciscan friend, said in his homily, "We come to bury his voice, but not his spirit, his hands, but not his works, his heart but not his love." He said Mychal had to be the first registered casualty because God needed his services to greet "the boys" on the other side, with his arms outstretched.

"He'll greet them with that big Irish smile and say, 'Hello, welcome. I want to take you to my Father!'"

THEA BOWMAN

The beauty and comfort of the Mystical Body of Christ is that we are all part of it. All of us have unique gifts; God has put a seal on each of us and calls us each by name. And just as a body needs noses and knees and belly buttons and laughter to be complete, so too we fit into the Mystical Body exactly where we are needed, using our gifts and doing the work only we can do, none better or lesser, all of equal importance to God.

At least that is how it *should* be. Sadly, being human and imperfect, we make hurtful judgments, considering some people of more value than others. This happened on a large scale in America over a century ago, when people owned other people and considered them their slaves. They were often churchgoing, Bible-reading, God-fearing people, who saw nothing wrong in calling themselves Christians and owning slaves.

Now we wonder how such a thing could ever have been. And yet today many of our black neighbors and friends still do not know true freedom and acceptance. Even in our church, African Americans want to share the wealth of their traditions, music and spirituality, only to find their gifts unwelcome or ignored.

But thanks to one black and beautiful nun named Thea Bowman, things are changing. She has moved people's minds and hearts—which is much more difficult than moving mountains—to see the truth and to act rightly and *joyfully*.

You cannot write about Thea without thinking of the word that goes with her—joy. She was, it is said, even a joyful child. She was born Bertha Bowman in 1937 in Canton, Mississippi, the adored daughter and only child of Theo, a doctor, and Mary Esther, a teacher. She was the granddaughter of freed slaves.

Her father's workday stretched from dawn to dark to take care of his patients' needs (he was the only black doctor in the area), and her mother was so generous, she would give whatever she had to anyone who requested it. Their loving kindness and compassionate ways were observed and absorbed by Thea and repeated in her own life.

While she was in grade school, she chose to become Catholic. Thea had been greatly influenced by her teachers, the Franciscan Sisters of Perpetual Adoration, so much so that she decided to join their order after finishing high school. What a journey that must have been when she left Mississippi for the first time to travel far north to the sisters' motherhouse in La Crosse, Wisconsin!

After graduation from Viterbo College in Wisconsin, she went on to Catholic University in Washington, D.C., where she obtained a Ph.D. in English literature. She went back to teach at Viterbo for a while and then returned to her hometown, Canton, to teach at the Holy Child Jesus Elementary School, delighted that she could work with "my people."

Working with her people was very much part of God's plan using Thea's gift of "blackness." God led her into work with the Office of Intercultural Affairs in the diocese of Jackson, Mississippi, and on the faculty of the Institute of Black Catholic Studies at Xavier University, New Orleans. Along with the teaching, she preached, lectured, exhorted, sang and lit spiritual fires within the hearts of those who heard her.

In the midst of all this, she discovered she had cancer and lived with it for six years. On March 30, 1990, at the age of fifty-two, she died, in the same house she was born in.

These are the facts about Thea's life, her *seen* achievements of her life. Of even more value are her unseen gifts—planting seeds of self-esteem, confidence and pride in the heritage and spirituality of her own people; educating and enlightening the white church community to appreciate the special contribution of people of all colors.

Thea knew who she was and rejoiced in it. Her message was *black is beautiful*, and she made it her ministry to share this message. "What does it mean to be black and Catholic?" she was asked. "It means that I bring my black self to my fully functioning church. I bring my whole history, tradition, experience....I bring my African American song, dance, gesture, movement; preaching, teaching, healing; responsibility."

She wore the brilliant, colorful robes and turbans of her heritage and used African art and music. She sang gospel music and clapped and roused audiences until they too were singing and clapping, in the old-time tradition of black Christian churches.

In these churches, worship is a true community celebration. Everyone prays and sings with and for each other. And preaching is an exuberant telling of God-stories and connecting the story of the Bible with the history of black people. Singing is as necessary as preaching. Thea said, "Most black people believe that the Spirit does not descend without a song. Song opens the hearts of the people for the coming of God's spirit."

Wherever and whenever God gave her the opportunity, Thea preached her message of love and acceptance—"we are all God's children and there is room for all of us"—from television programs to college campuses and conferences of bishops. When she was asked, "How do you know if what you are doing is really for the Lord or just for the praise others give you?" she answered, "How are you going to know? Just go ahead and act and leave it up the Lord. The old folks had a prayer, 'Use me, Lord, use me.' So never worry...just do what you are doing and tell him to use you."

When cancer interrupted her mission of preaching, she had yet another gift to share with us: Suffering was also a way for her to say "use me, Lord."

"I know that God is using me in ways beyond my comprehension....As a sick person, I can listen. That's a ministry that many people hunger for. Active people often don't realize how important listening is. Whatever I can do, if I do it in Jesus' name, it's acceptable and satisfactory. I pray for people who are needy, who hurt, and who are alone, who are lonely. I pray for the ones who are discouraged and addicted. I pray for the many people who have asked for prayers....I pray that we may learn to reach across boundaries of race, nationality, class and status and love one another and help one another. I pray that we create a holy city where they will know us because we love one another."

She had no fear of death. "Death is just part of life—it's going home. We are marching towards home...the spiritual journey is the journey home. Home is where you're loved. It's where you belong. In the hard days and in the trying days, my people prayed for home. When I get home, I'm going to put on my robe and tell the story of how I made it over! I'm not going to die, honey, I'm going home like a shooting star!"

On March 30, 1990, Thea did go home. Can't you imagine the singing and the clapping and the *Hallelujahs* when she arrived? Maybe they welcomed her with one of her favorite spirituals:

> I've done some good
> I've done some wrong
> And now I go where I belong
> The Lord has willed it so
> He knows my heart and he knows best
> He will not harm what he has blessed
> And so I go to take my rest
> Where sweet wild roses grow!

A few days before her death, Sister Thea dictated these thoughts on making the days of Holy Week truly holy. They appeared in an article printed in the diocesan paper of Jackson, Mississippi:

Let us resolve to make this week holy...by living grateful, faithful, prayerful, generous, just and holy lives.

Let us resolve to make this week holy by sharing holy peace and joy within our family...asking forgiveness for past hurts and forgiving one another from the heart.

Let us resolve to make this week holy by sharing holy peace and joy with the needy, the alienated, the lonely, the sick and afflicted, the untouchable. Let us unite our sufferings, inconveniences and annoyances with the suffering of Jesus. Let us stretch ourselves, going beyond our comfort zones to unite ourselves with Christ's redemptive work.

Let us be practical, reaching out across the boundaries of race and class and status to help somebody, offering to the young an incentive to learn and grow, offering to the downtrodden resources to help themselves. May our fasting be the kind that saves and shares with the poor, that actually contacts the needy, that gives the heart to heart, that touches and nourishes and heals.

During this Holy Week when Jesus gave his life for love, let us truly love one another.

THE HOLY INNOCENTS OF 9/11

If you add together all those lost in the terrorist attacks in New York City, Washington, D.C., and the field of Pennsylvania, you would have enough people to make a small village. And in this village, you would have a blending of humanity. Mothers, fathers, daughters, sons, husbands, wives, grandparents. Catholics, Jews, Baptists, Buddhists, Muslims, Unitarians, Atheists. Cooks, waiters, window-cleaners, stockbrokers, receptionists, lawyers, secretaries, artists, scientists, teachers, firefighters, policemen.

And everyone would have a story. People on the planes going to weddings, graduations, college, vacations. People in the Towers going to their jobs on a sunny autumn day, drinking their coffee, telling jokes, making plans for the weekend. They were today's Holy Innocents, bystander victims of the scheme of minds crazed with hate.

Over and over we are reminded of the savagery humans can inflict upon one another, from the time Herod killed all the male babies, the Holy Innocents, under the age of two in Bethlehem, in his mad desire to slay the Christ child. In all the centuries since, through the atrocities of wars, the German concentration camps, the massacres in Rwanda, the Oklahoma City bombing, the Innocents are the ones who die because they are in the way.

It is impossible for us humans to understand why such things happen. It isn't that we believe God looks away and doesn't care. It's just that he knows and we don't. As Father. Mychal says about sudden death, "There are really no answers that you can give people, but somehow you have to give them hope that somewhere, something good will come to lift us up and keep us going until we get the eternal vision of God. The closer tragedy is to heart and home, the more likely faith is to form, because we've been tried and tested...."

What may have lifted the broken hearts of those families left behind was the certainty that their loved ones live, and live radiantly. How that September sky must have been filled with the homecoming of souls and their companion angels, a celestial traffic jam with welcomers in Heaven eager to receive the travelers!

A poem by Henry Van Dyke tells of a ship sailing off until only a speck can be seen on the horizon, and those waving her off sigh, "There, she's gone." At that moment, there are other eyes watching her coming and other voices ready to take up the glad shout, "There she comes!"

This is how it must have been for the Holy Innocents of September 11, 2001, with God and all the saints and heroes waiting to greet them with a "Look, here they come!"